NATURAL THEOLOGY,

OR

THE EXISTENCE, ATTRIBUTES

AND

GOVERNMENT OF GOD.

INCLUDING

THE OBLIGATIONS AND DUTIES OF MEN,

DEMONSTRATED BY ARGUMENTS DRAWN FROM THE PHENOMENA OF NATURE.

BY

LUTHER LEE, D. D.

Professor of Theology and Biblical Literature in Adrian College, Adrian, Michigan.

"The works of the Lord are great, sought out of all them that have pleasure therein."

"The heavens declare the glory of God; and the firmament showeth his handy-work."

SYRACUSE:
WESLEYAN METHODIST PUBLISHING HOUSE.
1866.

Wm. J. Moses, Printer, Auburn, N. Y.

CONTENTS.

PREFACE.

This volume is the result of the Author's conviction of the need of such a work. On being called to teach in the department of Natural Theology, he found no Text-Book in use in the Institution, and on inquiry, none was found in the market, which appeared to be sufficiently adapted to the instruction of a class in College, to justify its introduction. The consequence was, the work of instruction was undertaken by means of original Lectures. This process revealed what all experienced teachers have found to be true; namely, that it is difficult for most students to come to their recitations with good lessons, from the hearing of a Lecture, read to them one or two days previously, without a Text-Book, that they can carry with them into their private study. To remove this difficulty, the Lectures, first read to a class, have been revised, and published in this convenient form.

On the subject of merit, the Author will leave these brief pages to speak for themselves, only stating that they teach what he earnestly believes, and that he intends nothing but good in giving them to the public.

It will be observed by every attentive reader, both Christian and Skeptic, that it has been the Author's design to elaborate a system of Natural Theology, in harmony with Revealed Religion. This appears to him to be best calculated to secure the two most important ends to be reached by any systematic embodiment of the principles of Natural Theology.

1. If the effort shall prove a success, a clear exhibition of the harmony between Natural and Revealed Religion, will remove much prejudice against Natural Theology as a science, and exalt it in the estimation of the Christian public.

2. Such an exhibition of Natural Theology will tend to lead Skeptics, who are interested in the study of Natural Religion, to examine the Scriptures, by which they will be compelled to admit that the Scriptures teach the truth, so far as Natural Religion reaches, or that their boasted Reason plays falsely. The Author is a believer in the Divine Inspiration of the Scriptures, and has made them the subject of his most intense study for half a century. Of course he cannot ignore his Christian faith, in writing a small treatise on Natural Theology.

With these remarks, his work is committed to the judgment of a candid public, hoping that it will be found, as the Author intends it, to promote truth, and supply a want in our Educational Interests.

LUTHER LEE.

ADRIAN COLLEGE, ADRIAN, Michigan, Jan. 1, 1866.

NATURAL THEOLOGY.

LECTURE I.

THE SCIENCE DEFINED, THE FIELD IT OCCUPIES MARKED OUT, AND ITS UTILITY INDICATED.

I. *The Science of Natural Theology Defined.*

The word Theology is derived from two Greek words, *Theos*, God, and *Logos*, Discourse ; hence, Theology denotes a discourse relating to God ; but in usage, it signifies the science which treats of the existence, attributes, character and government of God, including the obligations and duties of men as God's creatures, and the subjects of his moral government.

The word Natural, as a prefix to Theology, stands opposed to Supernatural ; hence, Natural Theology is the science of God, as derived from the revelations of Nature, without a supernatural revelation, such as is believed to be contained in the Scriptures. If the Scriptures are true, and have been derived in the manner which they claim for themselves, they give us a supernatural Theology. But any Theology which may be learned from the works of God, without any such supernatural revelation as the Scriptures claim for themselves, is properly called Natural Theology, because it is a revelation of Nature, or a revelation of God in Nature. If the human intelligence cannot find God revealed in some or all of the phenomena of Nature, there can be no such thing as Natural Theology. If the human intelligence can find God revealed in all or in any part of the phenomena of Nature, so much of God as is thus revealed constitutes the substance, extent, and limits of Natural Theology. Natural Theology, then, supposes that the works of God are a revelation of himself to the human mind, and proceeds to demonstrate and interpret such revelation, by which process the science is elaborated.

From what has been said, it follows that the object of Natural Theology is to make us acquainted with God, that we may know that He is, and what are His attributes, character and government, and what obligations we are under to Him. This being the case, the whole science is involved in two questions, namely :

1. Is God so revealed in His works as to enable the human intellect to gain, through this source, with reasonable certainty, such a knowledge, in kind and degree, as renders the science useful and important ?

2. If God may be known through His works, that is, through what is known as the phenomena of Nature, what and how much of Him may be thus known? These two questions appear to bring before us the whole subject of Natural Theology, and to elaborate answers to them, is the task of him who would construct a science on the subject.

II. *The Field of Investigation marked out.*

In prosecuting our inquiry after the truth of Natural Theology, we shall find the whole field of Nature open before us, and in this field must the truth be found, if found at all. We are not limited to any part of this field; its wide extent is open before us, comprehensive of all the objects of human knowledge. The proof may be found in the harmonious complex whole, or in any part or parts of that whole; and in either case the conclusion will be equally certain, if the process of reasoning be sound. As the same mind is not likely to comprehend all the departments of Nature to the same extent, it must be expected that there will be divisions and classifications of the evidence, and that each investigator will contribute his portion of the proof from his own department of science.

1. Those principally devoted to the study of Physical Geography will be most likely to find proofs of the existence of God on the broad surface of the earth. If they can see foot-prints of the Creator, or marks of an Almighty forming hand

impressed upon the face of the world, they will report to us, as the result of their research, that there is a God. If rocks talk in reason's ear of the hand that moulded them ; if brooks and rills sing to the reasoning soul of man, the praise of the Immortal Spirit that bids their waters flow with unabating fullness ; if mountains are suggestive of the power that reared them as Nature's watch-towers ; if the eye of reason can see the touch of a Divine hand in the flowers that bloom, and in the golden fruits as they ripen ; and if the heart of gratitude conceives the idea of a bountiful Provider, on sight of rich and abundant harvests waving on hill and plain, there is furnished from this department an array of corroborating proofs conclusive of the existence of God, provided the facts are clear, and the conclusions well drawn from the premises.

2. The Astronomer directs his way upward, and wanders in thought amid celestial spheres, and as he traces the rounds of revolving worlds, he notes the response which world gives to world, and system to system ; by which the motion of each is modified, controlled, and perpetuated, and the grand galaxy of worlds is held in its glorious array, and rolled on in its cycles. If such a view of the universe suggests to the beholder a higher Power, leading to the conception of a Creator, who made and governs the whole, there is developed the truth of Natural Theology ; and Addison, when under the

influence of the conception, he uttered the following, gave us not only poetry, but the truth of philosophy :

> "The spacious firmament on high,
> With all the blue ethereal sky,
> And spangled heavens, a shining frame,
> Their great Original proclaim:
>
> "In reason's ear they all rejoice,
> And utter forth a glorious voice;
> Forever singing as they shine,
> 'The hand that made us is divine.'"

This is as good Theology as it would be if it were derived from any other source, provided the conception is the legitimate consequence of the contact of the knowing mind with these vast ethereal objects of knowledge.

3. The Geologist is likely to dig for the great truth of the Divine existence, and if he can find the proof folded in the various strata, it is just as good as though he brought it from above, provided his premises are facts, and not assumptions, and his conclusions are logical deductions.

4. There is one department of Nature yet unnamed, in which search may be made for the great idea. The Mental Philosopher may search within himself, and in so doing will find his own mind its greatest wonder to itself. The mind is a knowing power, a power to know ; and yet it does not know itself. It knows itself to be a knowing power, and yet it knows not what the power is that knows. It

knows itself to be a spirit, because it knows that matter knoweth not. It knows its own identity, that it is the same continued self, because it knows that that which now knows is that which knew in time past ; and yet what is the essence, the substance in which this same continued power to know resides, it does not know.

The mind, in consciousness, knows its own thoughts, and purposes, and feelings, and in knowing so much, it knoweth all its knowledge. It is hid from itself under an impenetrable veil of mystery, which defies the gaze of its own piercing eye, and yet looks out upon the world and sees much, and gathers in its store of knowledge from near and far. It walks through the earth in thought, and ascends the milky way, and surveys the heavens, and leaps from world to world, and so comprehends the motions of the heavenly bodies for a hundred years to come, as to tell the year, and day, and hour, and minute, when each eclipse, and other celestial phenomenon, will transpire. In a word, the mind grasps this vast universe of worlds, and wraps the whole up in one of its little complex thoughts, which a mental Philosopher would call an understanding notion, and holds the whole under its own eye of reflection. If the mind, which possesses such intellectual powers, does, in the exercise of these powers, awaken within itself the conception of a higher creative power, by which the soul says to itself, there must be a Creator, who made me to know, and made all the objects of my knowledge, there is found a volume of Theology within ; provided the conception is the result of the mind's own spontaneity, under the pressure of its surroundings.

It is not affirmed that all that has been supposed will be found in exact conformity with the above outline ; that would be to regard the question as settled. The design, thus far, has not been to demonstrate the truth of Natural Theology, but only to point out the field in which we are to search for it, and open up the way so plainly that we shall not wander from the right path, in our investigations.

III. *The Utility of the Science Defended.*

In entering upon a consideration of this question, it is proper to premise that there are three classes of opinions to be met in the investigation, namely, all Christians who receive the Scriptures as given by inspiration of God, all Deists, who reject the Scriptures as a Revelation from God, yet believe in the existence of a Supreme Creator, and Ruler of the Universe ; and Atheists, who deny the existence of God, and admit of no intelligence higher than their own. These three classes, viewing the subject from such widely different stand-points, sustain different relations to the question of utility, and the question needs to be discussed with special reference to each of the three separately.

1. *Is the Science useful, allowing Christianity to be true?*

There is not a uniformity of opinion on the subject. Some have assumed, that if Natural Theology be admitted as a Science, sufficiently comprehensive and clear to render its study useful and important, it must detract from the necessity, importance and usefulness of the Scriptures. The argument is, that the fact that God has given us a revelation of His will in the Scriptures is proof positive that such a revelation is necessary in our circumstances, and if a revelation is necessary, it follows that Natural Theology is insufficient, and therefore unimportant, if not useless, with those who possess the Scriptures. This may appear plausible upon its face, yet it admits of a sufficient reply.

First. The study of Natural Theology, if rightly pursued, cannot fail to support and illustrate much of the evidence by which we labor to support the claim of the Scriptures to Divine Inspiration. Allowing all that is claimed for the Scriptures, still the undeniable fact will remain, that many do not believe and never have believed and appreciated them, and by such they are regarded as false or fabulous. A portion of this class maintain the sufficiency of Natural Theology, and urge it as opposed to and contradictory of the Scriptures. This no Christian can allow, and his only sure ground of defence against it is, the study of Natural Theology, that he may understand it, and make it talk its own truthful language, and not allow it to be palmed off as the voice of Nature, distorted by the blind heart and false tongue of Infidelity. If God is alike the Author of the material universe and of the Scriptures, they must speak the same language, so far as they speak on the same subject. God has not spoken one thing through Nature, and something different and contradictory through the Scriptures. They may speak different truths, but cannot speak contradictory truths, for one truth cannot contradict another truth. Where there is contradiction, there is falsehood. All real science is truth, and hence there must be perfect harmony between Science and the Scriptures, upon the assumption that the Scriptures are a revelation from God. But science is often imperfectly understood, and that which has been regarded as science has, on further investigation, been found to be error. Thus has there often been contradiction between what was at the time regarded as science and the teachings of the Scriptures; and again and again has Skepticism brought forward its own scientific ignorance, to refute the clearly demonstrated truths of Revelation; but in every case, further investigation has developed a scientific error, or a misapplication of truth, which has left our faith in the Scriptures resting upon a firmer foundation than before. If the Scriptures are a Revelation from God, their voice must accord with the voice of Nature, so far as they both speak on the same subject. If, then,

Natural Theology, on investigation, proves to be a practical science, and is found to teach the same truths that are taught in the Scriptures, so far as it teaches anything, then will natural and revealed religion not only harmonize, but will mutually support and explain each other; and the study of Natural Theology may be of great service to the cause of Scriptural religion.

Second. If all be admitted that is or can be claimed for Natural Theology, allowing its widest range, it cannot, in the slightest degree, supercede the necessity, or lessen the importance of the Scriptures. Allowing that Natural Theology can make us acquainted with the existence of God, and our general obligation to obey Him in the light of the simple relation existing between Creator and created intelligences, it would not meet our religious wants, and the Scriptures would still be necessary. Our relation to God is not the simple relation between a Creator and created intelligences. We are revolted, fallen beings, redeemed, and under a dispensation of grace, upon which subjects Natural Theology does not and cannot teach, when all its claims are allowed. Our condition, as fallen beings, requires a remedial system, in regard to which Natural Theology is necessarily silent, that system being found only in the Gospel. It has now been shown that Natural Theology may greatly assist the cause of Revealed Religion, while, by no possibility can it lessen its importance; and here let the Christian aspect of the subject be dismissed.

2. *Deists who reject the Scriptures as a Revelation from God, must admit the utility of Natural Theology.*

Deists, at least the better class of them, while they deny the Inspiration of the Scriptures, believe in the existence of God, and to some extent in Natural Religion. Natural Theology is all the Theology they admit; and holding, as they generally do, that the light of Nature is sufficient, they must admit the utmost importance of the science of Natural Theology, well systematized and clearly developed. Such a system of Natural Theology may be useful to them, not only by making them better men, as Deists, but by leading them to embrace Christianity, by revealing to them the entire harmony of Natural Theology, when properly understood, with Revealed Religion.

3. *Natural Theology may benefit Atheists.*

Atheists deny that there is any such being as God, in the Theistic sense. With them, Nature is all. As they deny everything but what they are pleased to call Nature, it is difficult to see how they can be reached, except by arguments drawn from Nature. They may be expected to contest the conclusions of Natural Theology, at every stage in the progress of its development; yet are they bound to investigate the subject, and cannot consistently refuse to give it their attention, for two very obvious reasons.

First. The principal issue is with them, and they cannot, as honest men, refuse to meet it. Is there a God, an Allwise and Almighty Being, before Nature, above Nature, and the Creator of Nature? Theists affirm, Atheists deny, and with them the issue is joined in Natural Theology.

Second. The appeal is to their only volume, Nature, and they must not turn away their ears when we read their own book. If they will attend to the argument, they may be convinced.

LECTURE II.

THE PRINCIPAL ISSUE STATED—THE ARGUMENT OPENED—THE TRUTH OF ETERNAL SELF-EXISTENCE ESTABLISHED—THE ADVANTAGES OF THE POSITION POINTED OUT.

I. *The Principal Issue Stated.*

The existence of God is the first great truth to be established in the process of elaborating a system of Natural Theology. There are two forms of error with which issue is joined, and which will be overthrown by the establishment of this truth.

1. It takes issue with Atheism, which denies that there is a God. This form of error has no system, and contains but one fundamental principle in its creed, and that has only a negative existence. That principle is, that there is no God. In the place of the common belief in the existence of God, it gives us nothing. To account for the various phenomena which it cannot overlook or deny, it sometimes talks of chance, sometimes of the efficiency of nature, and sometimes of the eternity of matter. These assumptions need not be examined and refuted at this point, as they will be over-

thrown by the establishment of the fact that there is a God.

2. The great affirmative proposition, that there is a God, takes issue with all forms of Pantheism. This name comes from two Greek words, *Pan*, all, and *Theos*, God, literally, *all God.* The doctrine of Pantheism is, that nature is God, God is every thing, and every thing is God ; every separate part is God, while the whole complex universe is the supreme God. This system was originated by the so-called Greek Philosophers, in their heathen blindness, but it constitutes the warp and woof of modern Transcendentalism.

In opposition to these errors the Theistical view stands opposed, which is, that there is a God, who is an eternal, almighty, intelligent Spirit, the Creator of all things besides Himself. The simple fact that there is a God must first be established, and then we shall have a ground on which we can show His character.

II. *The Argument Opened.*

To furnish a ground upon which we can stand and elaborate direct arguments in support of Theism, it is necessary to establish the fact of eternal self-existence somewhere, as a necessary truth. Something is, and of necessity must be, eternal.

1. Nothing cannot produce something. This is so self-evident that no one is likely to deny it. To affirm that nothing can produce something, is to

affirm that nothing is something. That which produces must be, must exist, and that which exists is something, not nothing. The word nothing, *no-thing*, is exclusive of every thing, and implies the absence of every thing, all matter, all spirit, all action, and all power to act ; and therefore nothing cannot produce something. To produce something implies the presence of both power and action, but nothing excludes them both ; therefore, where nothing is, something cannot be produced. If there had once been nothing, no matter when, there never could have been any thing.

The same result will be reached by the application of another self-evident truth. No one will, or can, deny that every effect must have a cause, and that it cannot transpire without the existence of such cause ; but nothing is not and cannot be a cause, since it is exclusive of every thing, and therefore, where nothing is, there can be no cause of any thing. A cause is something and not nothing, and as a cause is not nothing, nothing cannot be a cause. The inevitable conclusion is, that where nothing is, nothing must remain, and something can never be. If, then, there had ever been a time when there was nothing, nothing would always have remained, and there never would have been any thing. If, then, there is now any thing, something has always existed, because something could not begin to exist without the prior existence of something else as its cause. As a cause is something, and must exist before an effect can exist, to say that something began to exist, when nothing existed, would be to make the self-contradictory affirmation that something existed when nothing existed.

2. There is something, that is, something now exists. The argument of Descartes proves this point, though it came far short of filling the measure of his proposed theory. He said, "I think, therefore, I am." Every rational person can affirm this with the greatest confidence. Every person knows, in consciousness, that he thinks, and his reason affirms that that which thinks, exists and is something. A class of Philosophers, called Idealists, have denied the existence of a material world, external to the human mind; but these intellectual dreamers have been constrained to admit the existence of mental phenomena, while they contend that nothing else is certain. This admission is sufficient for the present argument, inasmuch as mental phenomena cannot exist without the existence of mind. Mental phenomena is something, and it implies the existence of mind, which is something, and its existence implies a cause why the phenomena is developed, when and what it is, and such cause must be something. How futile is it, then, to insist that nothing exists. No man can prove to himself that there is absolutely nothing in existence, he can do no more than doubt, and that which doubts must exist. No man can evade the fact of his own existence, for if he denies it, by that very denial he proves it, for

that which denies must exist. The second premise in the argument is then proved, which is, that something exists.

3. Something must have always existed. This conclusion follows from the two preceding propositions, which have been established with absolute certainty. Nothing cannot produce something; something now is; therefore, something always was. We have now reached a position in the argument where it is certain that something has, and of necessity must always have existed, and is eternal. The question here is not, what is eternal, which is eternal, whether little or much, or all, is eternal, but simply that something is, and of necessity must be, eternal, and so far, the preceding argument is and must be, absolutely conclusive.

It is not pretended that the Theistic view of God has been proved, nor even the Deistic view, but a position has been established, upon which other arguments can be built, bearing directly on the point.

III. *The Advantages of the Position pointed out.*

The simple point that something must be eternal, which has been established, may, at first sight, appear but a small gain, yet it will prove like an elevated outpost, which, when taken, will silence every other battery, and command the whole city.

1. The fact proved that something is eternal, gives us the advantage ground of self-existence, not only as a possible thing, but as an absolute fact

existing in the elemental nature of some thing or being. That which always existed was never caused to exist, and hence can have no cause of existence, beyond such uncaused cause as exists in its own eternal nature; and that which has no cause of existence, only what exists in itself, is, and must be, self-existent. The argument proves, beyond the power of a doubt, that self-existence is not only possible, but that it has an embodiment in some thing or being that really is. This self-existent something or being, whenever and wherever we shall find and identify it, we propose to call God, the Creator, the Jehovah. The advantage of the position, in part, lies in the fact that it will preclude future cavil as the argument progresses. It being proved that something is eternal, and consequently self-existent, all future cavil about the impossibility and absurdity of self-existence is precluded, and we may carry the principle forward in the argument, and search out and identify the Eternal One, and Atheism will be overthrown.

2. The position gained that something must be eternal, will enable us to overthrow all forms of Pantheism, and every other like ism, by simply proving that Nature had a beginning. If it can be proved that the material universe had a beginning, it will follow that there was a cause for the beginning, which existed before Nature, and which, itself, must be uncaused and eternal, in which case Nature cannot be God, and Pantheism will be proved false.

In connection with every index, which reason finds in all the field of Nature pointing to a beginning, she affirms, clearly and absolutely, that there was a cause of that beginning, which was itself uncaused and eternal, which annihilates the Pantheistic view.

3. The point proved that something must be eternal, will greatly assist us in our search after God, and in identifying Him when we find Him revealed in any of His works. We may trace backward chains of causes and effects, as they are stretched through the ages of the past, and may find footprints and hand-marks of the Great First Cause, but He is not found in any succession of causes and effects, for these must all have had a beginning, and yet something is eternal, and that must be looked for back of all successions. Every succession of cause and effect may point reason back to God, as the great universal cause of all, but none of them is God himself, for as He is eternal, He must exist back of all successions. What we call time, is duration measured by the revolutions of the heavenly bodies, hence time is known to man, only as duration measured and divided into periods by events, and as we trace the stream of time upward to its source, the events by which it is measured and divided into successive periods must grow less, until we reach the first event where time began, and here we find the Great First Cause of all things, Himself uncaused, self-existent, dwelling in His own eternity. All along the course of time, and in the

motions of the orbs that measure time, and in every thing that time evolves, we may be able to find proofs of the existence of an Eternal One, but Him we find not in person or substance, in any thing that had a beginning, in any thing that is marked by change, in any thing that increases the number of its years, nor yet in any thing that shall have an end. When, in thought, we follow backward the indexes which time has set up along her course, to point to her beginning, until we reach the place where time herself was first evolved, as the worlds wheeled into their orbits and formed the grand galaxy; here we pause in awe, and know that all beyond is the Eternal One, dwelling in His own infinitude of self-existence.

LECTURE III.

THE VISIBLE UNIVERSE HAD A BEGINNING.

I. *The Issue Defined.*

At this point in the investigation, a new issue is raised. In the preceding argument the issue was, is there something which is eternal, which always existed, which never began existence ; or did every thing have a beginning ; or is there nothing now ? It was demonstrated that something is eternal. That being settled, a new one is raised, by taking an advanced step in the general argument, which is, what and which is eternal ? is all eternal, or is there an eternal Creator, who is the cause of all existence except his own ? This issue is between Atheism and all forms of Pantheism, on one side, and Theism on the other. Atheism and Pantheism agree in affirming that the visible Universe is eternal, while Theism denies it, and affirms that there is an Eternal, Intelligent Being, commonly called God, who created the visible universe. The present argument regards only what is called the material universe, or matter.

II. *Time and Eternity Defined.*

To bring the argument out distinctly, and in its full force, it is necessary to define Time and Eternity, and make plain the distinction between them.

The subject of eternity has been greatly mystified, by attempted definitions and explanations. In these attempts, made by a number of able writers, two principal errors have been committed. The first is that of attempting to form an abstract notion of eternity, and then to treat of it and explain it accordingly, as an abstract something, separate from God, as though it were a place where God lives, or an element in which he lives. The second error lies in confounding this supposed notion of eternity with our notion of time, as though time were a part, and eternity the whole of the same thing. All this can only serve to mystify and produce confusion of thought. If time were a part of eternity, "a fragment broken off from eternity," as one author has called it, then eternity must consist of parts, and cannot be infinite or unlimited, as all agree that it is. No matter into how many parts it be divided, whether two or many, and no matter how large one part may be, and how small the other, relatively to each other, it is a self-evident truth, an intuition of reason, that no number of parts, each of which must be limited to be a part, can, combined, constitute an infinite, unlimited whole. It is then certain that time, being divided into limited periods, cannot be a part of eternity, unless eternity also be a limited period, divided into less periods.

No abstract idea can be formed of eternity. What is it in the abstract? It is not matter, for matter is limited, bounded, and divisible. It is not spirit, for there is but one Eternal Spirit, and that is the God of the Theist. It is nothing which God has created, for then it must have had a beginning, and cannot be eternal, and of course not eternity, as understood. It cannot be something separate from the being of God, which was never created, for then there would be two eternal natures, and God cannot be the Creator of all things, since there is this one thing, besides God, eternity, which never was created. It is clear, then, that there can exist in the human mind no abstract notion of eternity; it is indescribable, undefinable, inconceivable and unthinkable; it is an absolute nonentity.

It may be asked how the idea got into the mind. The reply is, it never did get into the mind, as an abstraction; it is not, never was, and never can be in the mind. We have the word eternity, but it represents no abstract idea. Webster defines the word eternity to be "duration, without beginning or end," but this definition is a solecism, for duration implies both limitation and lapse, or a passing onward, a continued increase of the whole period

2

of the duration referred to. Even Mr. Webster defines duration to be, "continuance in time," and when he adds, "everlasting duration," as expressing a shade of meaning within his one definition, he only affirms an endless continuance, but does not deny a beginning, which comes short of the common notion of eternity. But should it be allowed that eternity is endless duration, or rather duration without beginning or end, a contradiction in terms, still this is not definable, and is inconceivable, it is unthinkable. We cannot form an abstract idea of duration without beginning or end. We can give it no ground or form in thought, so as to hold it in the mind as an object of attention and reflection. It is not space, limited or infinite. It is not place, large or small. It is not a sentiment or a principle, as right and wrong, or beauty and deformity. It is not a principle or rule of action as a law. It is not body, and has no form, no locality, no extension, no quality, and must be absolutely unthinkable as an abstraction. What, then, is eternity? and how is it distinguished from time?

We give the only understandable definition of eternity, when we say that it is one of the divine attributes; that it is that element of self-existence, which renders the being of God without beginning and without end. The fact has been demonstrated, that something is eternal, by which is meant, without beginning or end. The fact of eternity, in this sense, has been proved, or rather shown to be a self-evident truth, an intuition of reason, but the attribute or quality of eternity, exists in God alone, and cannot be abstracted, and is unthinkable as an abstract notion. Eternity enters into our notion of God. We conceive of God as an Eternal Spirit, almighty, all-wise, omnipresent, just and good. Of such a being every one can conceive, and form a distinct understanding notion of him, embracing the above named attributes; the complex notion is clearly thinkable, while the manner is incomprehensible and unthinkable. The attribute or quality of eternity exists in God himself, and exists nowhere else, has no existence in any other being or thing, and hence is incapable of being abstracted, and is unthinkable as an abstraction. When we undertake to make an abstraction of eternity, and treat of it as a distinct being, thing, or entity, existing separate from God, as an element in which He has His being, yet not Himself, the mind becomes confused and lost in its attempt to explain what cannot be explained, to define what cannot be defined, and to think what cannot be thought.

We can now define time, and no one will fail to distinguish time, and all that time has evolved, from eternity, and to note the whole as devoid of the attribute of eternity.

Time is duration measured by the revolutions of the heavenly bodies. Time is known to us only by events. Our experience of successive sensible events, events known to sense, in connection with consciousness of personal identity or continued sameness, gives us an idea of time, the lapse of duration. Without events, no lapse could be perceived, and time would be unknown. The revolutions of the earth upon its own axis give us day and night, events by which time is measured. The revolutions of the earth around the sun, the centre of our system of worlds, give us another and larger measure by which time is divided into years.

III. *The principles applied, and the argument finished.*

It is obvious, from the definitions given, that the visible universe is not eternal, that time, which is known only in events, must have had a beginning with the whole machinery by which it is measured. The visible universe cannot have always existed, because its revolutions are increasing in number, and therefore must be limited, and must diminish as they are numbered backward along the course of time. It would be folly to affirm that the earth has made no more revolutions now, than it had when the Pyramids of Egypt were built. If then less years had elapsed when the Pyramids were built than at this date, there must have been still less at a date as remote from that as that is remote from this. Upon the same principle, the number of years must continue to decrease, until the first revolution of the earth is reached, where time began.

The whole of time can be no more than a succession of days and years, limited in number. Time being divided into parts, days and years, each limited, the whole of time must be limited. Every part being less than the whole, must be limited, and as all the parts are limited, the whole must be, for no number of limited parts can make an unlimited whole. Time is then limited, and must have had a beginning, and of course the visible Universe must have had a beginning, and consequently cannot be eternal.

The question here is not, how old this earth is, nor yet how old the Universe is of which it is a part, whether six thousand years, or six hundred thousand, or six hundred millions. As each revolution sustains to all the revolutions the relation of a part to a whole, all the revolutions must be limited; and combined, can constitute but a limited period; and as the existence of the orbs is measured by their revolutions, the whole system must have had a beginning.

IV. *Thus far Natural Theology testifies to the truth of Biblical Theology.*

In elaborating a system of Natural Theology, it is no part of the work to vindicate the claims of the Scriptures to Divine Inspiration, nor even to expound them; but to show that Natural Theology is in harmony with the teachings of the Scriptures, is the legitimate and indispensable work of him who would elaborate a system of Natural Theology, with any hope of success, so far as the Christian world is concerned. This shall be done, in connection with every fundamental truth which our Natural Theology is made to teach. Let it not be said that there is a departure from the legitimate work of teaching Natural Theology, when it is shown to be in harmony with the Scriptures, by showing that they teach the same thing. Without such exhibition of a harmony between the two, either in the work itself, or in the mind of the reader, the best system of Natural Theology would fall powerless to the ground, in the presence of every Christian mind. The exhibition of such harmony is not to establish the claims of the Scriptures, but rather to vindicate Natural Theology against a prejudice which may exist in the minds of some believers in the Scriptures ; but more especially to relieve it of distortions and mis-applications of Infidels, by which they have labored to array Natural and Revealed Religion against each other.

After stating the reasons for the course to be pursued, it is proper to show that the conclusion reached by the preceding argument, is in perfect harmony with the Scriptures. As Nature, by every revolution, affirms a beginning, so the Scriptures declare that, "In the beginning, God created the heavens and earth."—Gen. i. 1.

Psal. cii. 26. "Of old hast thou laid the foundation of the earth, and the heavens are the work of thine hands." Rev. iv. 11. "Thou hast created all things." Chap. x. 6. "Who created heaven, and the things that therein are, and the earth, and the things that therein are, and the sea, and the things that are therein." The clear and undeniable teaching of the Scriptures is, that the visible Universe had a beginning. Its origin is pointed out when it said, "These are the generations of the heavens and the earth, when they were created, in the day that the Lord God made the earth and the heavens."—Gen. ii. 4.

LECTURE IV

MATTER IS NOT ETERNAL.

In the preceding Lecture it was demonstrated that the visible universe, as now organized, had a beginning, but the argument did not raise the question whether matter has or has not always existed in some form. The issue now raised is, Has matter always existed in some form, or had it a beginning. This issue will be seen, at a glance, to be a vital one, for if matter had a beginning, there must have been a cause for that beginning, an active, creative Power, which existed before matter, and that creative power is the God of the Theist. The issue is direct between Atheism and Theism. It is the one great object of Atheists to annihilate the God of the Bible, believed by the Theist to be an Eternal, Self-existent, Intelligent, Omnipotent Spirit, who created all things. As it is so clearly self-evident that something must be eternal, they affirm the eternity of matter as the only means of escaping the most terrible thought to them, that there is an Eternal God, to whom they are accountable for their conduct.

I. *The Position avails nothing to Atheism.*

1. It overthrows their principal objection to Theism. Atheists insist that it is impossible to conceive of an eternal God, who is uncaused, and who never began to be ; in a word, they affirm that we cannot conceive of a self-existing being. But when they are pressed with arguments drawn from the visible Universe, in proof that it had a Creator, they forget their difficulty of conceiving of self-existence, and affirm that the Universe is eternal. To say nothing of the inconsistency of this course, it is an admission that something is eternal, and self-existent, and leaves the issue a simple one on the question, is the visible Universe eternal and self-existent, or is there an eternal God who created it ? This gives the Theist the advantage of all the marks of design which Nature reveals, which design does not inhere in nature, as proof of the existence of an intelligent designer, which advantage will hereafter be pressed.

2. If it were admitted that matter is eternal, it would not relieve the Atheistic view. It was demonstrated in the preceding Lecture, that time and all that time has evolved, had a beginning, that the earth performed a first revolution. This renders it just as necessary to suppose the existence of God, as a means of accounting for that beginning of time, that first revolution of the earth, as it would be to account for the existence of matter,

upon the admission that matter is not eternal. The admission of the eternity of matter does not account for the present arrangement and mechanism of matter, as it exists in the machinery of the Universe. As this cannot have been eternal, as was proved, were it allowed that matter is eternal, it would still be necessary to suppose the existence of a God, to account for the present forms and arranged forces of matter.

3. It is much more consistent to suppose that there is a God, who created matter, and gave it all the forms it wears, by which we account for all the marks of intelligence impressed upon it, which intelligence matter itself does not possess, than to assert the eternity of matter, as a means of refuting the idea of the existence of a God ; by which all these marks of intelligence are left unaccounted for. Until the signs of intelligence, seen in the arrangements and developed forces of matter are accounted for, the existence of an intelligent Creator is just as much a necessary truth, after affirming the eternity of matter, as before ; the Atheist therefore gains nothing by this position.

II. *The assertion that matter is eternal is an assumption which does not admit of the slightest degree of proof.*

1. If matter be eternal, there can be no history of the fact ; no record can reveal the origin of that

which had no origin Nor can the fact be known that matter is eternal, if there be no Eternal God to reveal the fact. If there be a God, as Theists contend, and were matter eternal, God could reveal the fact of the eternity of matter, and it might thus be known ; but denying the existence of God, as Atheists do, they cannot pretend that the eternity of matter can, by any possible means, be known.

2. While it is impossible to prove the eternity of matter, if it had a beginning, that fact will admit of proof. Whether any such proof exists, or does not exist, it is entirely possible that such proof should exist. If matter was created, a record of that creation is a possible thing, whether any such record does exist or not ; or the fact of such creation might be communicated to man by the Creator, at any subsequent period ; or matter might be so arranged by the Creator as to show signs in itself of having had a beginning. It is therefore legitimate to attempt to prove that matter had a beginning, that it was created. In this issue, Theism occupies an advantage-ground, and Atheism a disadvantageous position. The Theistic side of the issue admits of proof; the Atheistic side does not admit of proof.

III. *The Issue explained as finally made up and joined.*

The issue in the present argument is made to turn on a particular science, and the question is, what does Geology teach in regard to the creation or eternity of matter? This issue has been raised by Atheists, and pressed in such a form as to put all Christians on the defensive.

1. Atheists being unable to prove that there is no God, and equally unable to adduce the smallest degree of proof that matter is eternal, occupy themselves with efforts to disprove and subvert the evidence usually relied upon as proof that the universe is the work of a Creator, God. They make their assault upon the Mosaic record of the creation of the world. As it must appear somewhat reasonable, that if there be a God who created all things, there should be given to men, in some way, an account of that creation; and as there is no such account which wears upon its face a semblance of truth, save the Mosaic record alone, that must be demolished, cost what it may. They have dug deep into the earth, and claim to have discovered from the different strata, each of which represents a distinct period in the history of the earth, that this world is much older than the Mosaic record makes it.

2. In reply to this, Christians make it their first work to defend their record. In reply, they say:

(1.) The 5865 years, which is the age of the world at this writing, according to the Mosaic record, commenced with the life of Adam, the first man.

(2.) If it be proved by Geology that the earth is

much older, it is no impeachment of the record. The record does not affirm that matter did not exist long before Adam. The record reads as follows:

" In the beginning God created the heavens and the earth. And the earth was without form and void ; and darkness was upon the face of the deep. And the Spirit of God moved upon the face of the waters." Gen. i. 1, 2.

How long the earth remained without form, and void, with darkness upon the face of the deep, before the Spirit of God moved upon the face of the waters, the record does not pretend to say. This may all have passed prior to the commencement of the six days employed in forming matter according to its present arrangements. The world may have lain in darkness, and void, or waste, as some render it, before God's Spirit moved upon it, long enough to account for all the changes which Geology indicates, and all this before the creation of Adam, with whom our account of time has its date. This exposition regards the words following as an independent statement of God's first act of creation, in which he created the material of the world, in a state of chaos : " In the beginning God created the heavens and the earth, and the earth was without form, and void, and darkness was upon the face of the deep." This enunciates the first act of creation, and describes the state that followed, as dark and waste. The exposition also regards the words following as the announcement of the commencement of the six days' work, subsequently described: "And God said, Let there be light, and there was light." From this point of beginning, the work proceeds until the whole is crowned by the creation of man. How long the dark, and void, or waste state existed, before the Omnific call for light, is not revealed in the Mosaic record, and if Geology has revealed that fact, it has only thrown so much light upon that record, without contradicting or impeaching it.

The Mosaic record being defended, we may attend to the final issue which the Atheist raises in his Geological argument. It is now narrowed down to a single question, namely, does the science of Geology indicate that the substance of the earth, matter, is eternal, or that it had a beginning? On this question the issue is now joined, and as the Atheist raised the issue, and forced it upon us, he cannot object to having his theory of the eternity of matter tested by it, or demur at any of the conclusions legitimately drawn from the discoveries of his favorite science of Geology.

IV. *What does Geology teach?—The Argument concluded—Matter proved to have been created.*

Geology simply proves a succession of changes, which the earth has undergone, and each change must have had a beginning, and points to a preceding state, until the first change which science can detect is reached, and at that point the creative act must have transpired, as will be proved.

1. Human remains are found only on or near the surface of the earth, beneath which change after change is clearly revealed in successive strata. This proves, beyond a doubt, that the human race is of recent origin, compared with the whole period of the earth's existence. One thing is now settled, and that is, man had a beginning, the human race is not eternal. Geology testifies that the earth existed, and that change after change was developed, requiring ages before man appeared.

2. As we descend towards the centre of the earth, we pass strata after strata, each requiring ages in the work of formation, until we pass below all animal remains. This makes two facts very plain. First, animals existed long before man, and secondly, animals did not exist until long after the earth existed. This proves beyond a doubt, that animal existence had a beginning, and is not eternal.

3. Still passing onward toward the centre, we find strata after strata, each representing an age or ages, until we reach a point below all vegetable remains. This proves that the earth existed long before vegetation existed, and consequently, that vegetation is not eternal, but had a beginning. There must have been a first plant and tree, or a number of each, which did not spring from previously existing plants and trees.

4. Still descending, we pass the limits of strati-

fication, and stand upon the primitive rock, the granitic mass, too deep for human exploration. This primitive rock, the last in the order of geological discoveries, is itself a crystallization, and must have had a beginning, a process involving time, and a completion.

5. The primitive rock, the last reached, is not only a crystallization, but a compound, and if we apply chemical analysis to it, until we reduce it to nature's simple elements, of which science has discovered between fifty and sixty, the end of scientific research will be reached, and we shall have approached the point where God began the work of creation, when he produced the elements, without form, void and dark.

The protracted argument may now be summed up in few words, and a final and certain conclusion reached. Every change which Geology proves to have taken place, in the structure of the earth, is suggestive of a beginning ; every strata bears upon its face marks of its lineal descent from the next below, and each rock is traced to its parent rock, until the ultimate rock is reached, and this being a crystallization, must have had a beginning, and its formations have transpired in time, and not in eternity. The whole process, if the teachings of Geology are reliable, proves that there must have been a beginning, a first state, and that was a state in time, and not an eternal state. If matter existed from eternity, in the simple state supposed, or indeed in any state, there could have existed no cause for change, and changes could never have transpired. If a cause for change had existed in matter from eternity, it would have acted from eternity, and there could have been no beginning of change, as proved. If no cause of change existed in matter from eternity, no cause for change could ever transpire, if there be no God, and matter would and must have remained without change. Matter, therefore, by the testimony of science, is proved to have had a beginning, and must have been created. Moreover, all the changes which matter has undergone, are scientific changes, science herself being witness. Science depends upon fixed laws, and law supposes a law-giver, and that law-giver must be the Author of Nature, and the God of the Theist; and the Atheistic theories of the eternity of matter, and of chance, and fortuitous circumstance, are all exploded. This is all in harmony with the teachings of the Scriptures, but this fact must be demonstrated in the succeeding Lecture.

LECTURE V.

MATTER WAS CREATED—ADDITIONAL ARGUMENTS—THE SCRIPTURES TEACH IN HARMONY WITH THE VOICE OF NATURE.

I. *The Previous Argument—Additional Arguments proposed.*

1. In the previous Lecture, Atheism was met upon its own chosen ground, and vanquished with its own selected weapon. It made its appeal to science, and by its own favorite science it has been overthrown. But while Atheism has depended almost or quite exclusively upon Geology for the overthrow of the Christian faith, and has itself been overthrown by it, there remain various other considerations which prove with equal conclusiveness that matter was created. Some of these shall be adduced in the present Lecture. These arguments will not only refute Atheism, as such, but every form of error which affirms or implies the eternity of matter, or denies that it was created. This appears necessary, in order to clear the subject of every embarrassment, as some Christian writers have expressed themselves in an equivocal manner on the

subject, if not in a manner which implies the eternity of matter, and thereby yield up every argument drawn from the visible Universe, in support of the existence of God.

II. *False Views corrected.*

Before entering upon the direct line of argument, it is proper to notice some views which have been advanced, judged to be erroneous. It may not be affirmed that any Christian writer of note, has, in so many words, affirmed that matter is eternal, that God did not create it ; but the following language of President Mahan appears to overlook the fact that God created the matter of the Universe.

"Does creation reveal its author as Infinite and Perfect ? Can an effect, acknowledged to be finite, reveal its cause as infinite ? If so, this revelation cannot be found in the mere *extent* of the Divine works. Suppose that the creation of *one* world only could have revealed its author as finite, how many such worlds would it take to reveal Him as infinite ? Nothing short of a number absolutely infinite, which is an absurdity. It is the highest absurdity, therefore, to reason, as is commonly done, from the mere *extent* of creation, which is still acknowledged to be finite, to the absolute infinity and perfection of its Author." *Intellectual Philosophy, page* 454.

A few remarks will render the errors contained in the above extract visible. The quotation has not been made for the purpose of attacking the respected author, but because it represents a view of the subject which appears to diminish greatly the force of any and all arguments drawn from the visible creation, if it will not overthrow them all, if fully admitted.

1. It mistakes the true ground of argument in the premises. It is not common, as affirmed, to reason from the extent of creation, in favor of the existence of God, but from the fact of creation. Creation in any visible extent, gives evidence in favor of the existence of an Infinite Creator, because reason cannot conceive that anything less than Infinity could produce a small creation. If appeals are made to the extent of creation, it is to move the mind by a view of the greatness of the Divine display, rather than as proof of the Infinity of the Creator.

2. The position is entirely unsound, that a finite creation cannot furnish proof of an Infinite God. It is admitted that creation, comprehensive of all known worlds, is finite, yet it may furnish proof of an Infinite Creator. Reason may affirm, intuitively, that Infinite Power alone can create. Nothing short of Infinite Power could create this one world we inhabit ; this world is not eternal, but was created ; therefore, there must be an Infinite Creator. The supposition "that the creation of one world would only have revealed its author as finite," is an absurdity on its face, because creation can be the work of nothing less than Infinite Power. It is admitted that if a finite power could create one world, the

existence of no number of worlds could prove their Creator Infinite; but the idea that a finite power can create the one world, is an assumption in contradiction of reason, in support of which no proof can be offered, of any kind or degree.

3. If it were true, as affirmed, that "nothing short of a number of worlds, absolutely infinite," could reveal their creator "as infinite," no possible proof can exist of Infinitude, and the Infinite is not and cannot be revealed to the human mind. If a finite creation cannot prove the existence of an Infinite Creator, it must be because Infinite proof is required to establish the fact that there is an Infinite God. If so, the fact of an Infinite God cannot be known to man. No adequate evidence can be adduced. The human mind being finite, it can neither receive or comprehend Infinite proof, and God cannot reveal himself to man only by finite proof. God can make only a finite revelation to the human mind, and the revelation he has made, is no more than finite, though it reveals the fact of an Infinite God. The human mind may comprehend a revelation of the fact that God is Infinite, while the infinitude itself is incomprehensible, and remains unrevealed to, or is hid from the mind. It is on no other principle that the existence of an Infinite God can be proved to, and be comprehended by, the human mind, without being itself infinite, and hence, to allow the position that a finite creation cannot reveal an Infinite God, would be to allow that no proof can exist of the

fact that God is Infinite, relatively to the human mind.

4. The language quoted from President Mahan, appears to overlook the fact, that God created the matter of the universe ; that is, produced it when and where there was nothing prior to such creation. This fact has been proved, and is about to be further proved by additional arguments. In the light of this fact, the existence of creation, the existence of one world, or many worlds, must reveal an Infinite Creator. There can be, on the part of finite power, no approach to the production of something, where there is nothing. No matter how frequently, and by what number you multiply any degreee of finite power, while it remains finite, as it always must, it can make no approach towards producing something where there is nothing ; reason revolts at the thought. It is certain, then, that the creation of one world, from nothing, or where nothing was, must reveal the Creator as Infinite, to the eye of reason.

III. *Direct Arguments in Proof that God created matter.*

1. There is and can be no direct proof of any kind or degree that God did not create matter, or that it is eternal.

This was shown in the preceding lecture, so far as Atheism is considered. It is only necessary to add, in this place, that it cannot be pretended that the Scriptures teach that matter is eternal, or that God did not create it.

Some have asserted that there is an absurdity in supposing that God could produce something where there was nothing, as negative proof that he did not create matter. This would be conclusive, if the denial that God could create matter was well founded, but of that there is no proof, nor does the nature of the case admit of proof. To prove that, would be to prove that Almighty power is not Almighty, that unlimited power is limited, that infinity is finite. Suppose we cannot conceive *how* God could create something where there was nothing; still we can conceive it possible that he should do it, just as easily as we can conceive that he should give to bodies of matter their forces, and so arrange those powers as to suspend systems of worlds in empty space, whirling from age to age with undiminished momentum; or that he should give to the load-stone its inexplicable power of attraction.

But there is real difficulty attending the opposite view. To suppose that matter is eternal, is to suppose that there are two separate, eternal, self-existent, independent entities, occupying the same infinity. If matter is eternal, it must be self-existent, and if self-existent, it must be independent, for that which is self-existent, cannot exist dependently upon something else.

Here, then, is a difficulty at which reason must stumble. It is not possible to believe that there are two eternal, self-existent, independent elements, each occupying its own sphere of existence, as both must, to be eternal, and yet that one should act upon, modify and control the other. This is unreasonable, yea, impossible, because it is an absurdity, a contradiction. There is, then, not only no possible proof that matter is eternal, but the thing is an absurdity, and therefore unthinkable.

2. Creation includes the production of spirit, as well as matter, which cannot have existed from eternity, as matter is supposed to have done. The supposition is, that matter existed in a common mass, or in a state of chaos, and that God's creative work was that of separating, assorting and forming, and arranging the several formations into the complicated and harmonious universe. This is in harmony with the divisibility of matter, but the principle is wholly inapplicable to spirit, which is indivisible.

The Christian doctrine is, that there are angel spirits, and that every human being is spirit in his rational and moral nature. It is impossible that all these spirits should have existed from eternity, in a common mass, and that God divided that mass into all these individual spirits, as he is supposed to have divided and arranged matter in the formation of the universe, as it now appears. Every angel, and every human soul is one, and only one individual being, incapable of division. It is not true that all angels and all human souls are eternal ; nor can it be pretended that there existed from eternity a common mass of spirit, out of which God formed them, as he is supposed to have formed the universe out of previously existing matter. Each angel, and each of the first two human souls, must have been produced by separate acts of creation, in each of which something must have been produced where there was nothing. God has, then, in creating angels and human souls, produced something where there was nothing; for he created all things that are in heaven, and in earth, which includes both matter and spirit. As it is clear that God did produce spirits without a pre-existing element out of which he formed them, there can be no ground left on which to base a denial that he created matter. Moreover, he is affirmed to have created both matter and spirit, without notice of any distinction in the manner or sense in which it was done; and as it is clear that in the creation of spirits, he produced the substance as well as the form, the conclusion is legitimate, that he created matter in the same sense, and that in the creation of the universe, he gave existence to matter, which did not exist until His creative act called it into being.

3. The word create properly signifies the production of what did not before exist. It is not necessary to lumber the subject with Hebrew authorities, any amount of which might be adduced. Two citations will be as good as more. Gesenius, in defining the Hebrew word, *bah-rah*, renders Gen. ii. 3—

"which God created in making," and adds, "It is apparent that *bah-rah* implies the creation of something new, which did not exist." The word thus defined is the word used where it is said, "God created the heavens and the earth."

Roy defines the same word, *bah-rah*, thus: "He created, caused to exist, spring forth, as the world, from nothing."

It is not pretended that the word is not used in an accommodated sense, to denote various formations where there was no production of a new substance; all words are sometimes used in an accommodated sense, to denote less or more than their proper sense; even the name of the Supreme Being is so used. The thing claimed is, that had the inspired writer designed to assert that God produced the heavens and the earth from nothing, this is the word he would have used. There is no other one word in the Hebrew language which so clearly and forcibly expresses that idea.

4. The account of the creation of the heavens and the earth, clearly implies that God produced the matter of which they are composed. The process is described as consisting of several creative acts in regular succession, until the whole work was crowned by the production of man. The first creative act, as described, could have accomplished nothing beyond the production of matter. The words are: "In the beginning God created the heavens and the earth." This can mean

nothing, unless it be the production of matter. It cannot mean their formation out of previously existing matter, because no formation was effected. The earth, as yet, had no form, and therefore nothing could have been done beyond the production of matter. After this first creative act, it is said, "The earth was without form and void, and darkness was upon the face of the deep." As God's first creative act produced the earth without form, there was an act of creation back of all form, which could not have given form, and therefore it could have done nothing but produce matter, which was afterwards formed by other acts of the Creator, successively described. Thus is it seen that the Mosaic account of creation teaches that God created the matter of the world, as well as to give it form, which was done after the matter was created.

5. There is much force in the fact that in all the accounts given of creation, and in all the allusions to the visible works of God, there is not one intimation that anything uncreated ever existed, except God alone, or that there was anything existing previously to creation, out of which God made the world. Had the substance of the universe existed from eternity, it is hardly possible that there should be no allusion to the fact, in the various appeals to God's mighty power and glory, as revealed in and through the visible creation.

6. The idea that matter was not created, but eternal, appears inconsistent with God's repeated

and unqualified declaration of his absolute proprietorship in all things. If matter never was created, but has always existed, it must be self-existent, just as much so as God is, and must have existed independently of God. Its existence must have been as uncaused and unconditional as God's existence. In no sense could God be said to have any proprietorship in matter if it be eternal, for in that case it existed by itself and of itself, just as much so as God did. All that God can claim as his, is the forms and motions which he has impressed upon matter ; the substance is not his, and never can be, since it is self-existent, in no sense depends upon him for its existence, but is co-eternal with him. If matter is eternal and self-existent, it must forever remain so, and must always possess an unconditioned existence, independently of God, whatever forms and motions He may impress upon it.

But as we cannot conceive of matter as destitute of its essential qualities, which qualities render it capable of receiving and sustaining its forms and motions developed in the machinery of the universe, those qualities must be eternal also, if matter be eternal. This view would give God no credit for those qualities of matter which are regarded as necessary ; for if matter is eternal, all that is essential to matter must be eternal, and the conclusion must follow, that the mechanical skill is all that honors God in creation. It may be admitted that God has displayed great mechanical skill, in the manner in which he has arranged the elements of nature, which he found, with their necessary qualities and inherent forces, existing from eternity, ready for his hand ; but while this is allowed, the claim of God must end here, without any merit for the materials of which he constructed the universe. Not one item of these materials did God furnish, if matter be eternal.

7. The affirmation that God created the substance of the universe, which has been supported by so many arguments, in this and the preceding Lecture ; arguments which nature, reason and science have affirmed, with their united voice, is no less clearly and positively asserted in the Scriptures. In this view, nature, reason, science and Revelation harmonize. Of course, no labored biblical argument will be attempted, but enough shall be said to show the harmony between Natural and Revealed Religion in this particular.

"For by Him were all things created, that are in heaven and that are in earth, visible and invisible, whether they be thrones, or dominions, or principalities, or powers, all things were created by Him, and for Him ; and He is before all things, and by Him all things consist."—Col. i. 16, 17.

There are three points in this text worthy of special attention.

(1.) It is comprehensive of the creation of angels, and human souls ; indeed, of all spirits. These must have been created in substance, the essence of their elemental natures must have been produced, as they could have had no pre-existence in some unorganic form, as was shown in the second direct argument above.

(2.) It is affirmed that "He was before all things." All things include matter of all kinds; He was therefore before all matter. But He could not have been before matter, if matter always existed. God himself could not be before matter, if matter is eternal; matter, therefore, cannot be eternal, and must have been created.

(3.) It is affirmed that "by Him all things consist." Here, again, all things include matter; matter, therefore, consists by him. But if matter is eternal, it must be self-existent, and consists by, in and of itself, and cannot consist by Him.

"Through faith we understand that the worlds were framed by the word of God, so that things which are seen were not made of things which do appear."—Heb. xi. 3.

On this text, two remarks only need be offered.

(1.) If the worlds were made of pre-existing matter, that matter does now appear in the things that are seen; which things were made of that pre-existing matter; therefore, the apostle, by denying that the things which are seen were made of things which do appear, denies that they were made of pre-existing matter.

(2.) No Greek scholar will deny that the most proper rendering of the text is: "things that are seen were not made of things which *did appear.*" The idea is, that the visible creation, which is now seen, was not made out of what then appeared, what then existed, but out of what did not appear, or exist, until God then and there created it.

It having been proved that God created matter, as well as to give it the forms it wears, and the forces it develops, both reason and Revelation affirm that the grand visible display is, to the human mind, a revelation of the Divine Architect. "The invisible things of Him from the creation of the world are clearly seen, being understood by the things that are made, even His eternal power and Godhead."—Rom. i. 20.

This text overthrows the position taken in the quotation reviewed in a previous portion of this Lecture, that a finite creation cannot prove an infinite God. The things that are made, referred to in the text, are finite, and yet the apostle affirms, that by them are clearly seen and understood "His eternal power and Godhead;" and here Natural and Revealed Religion speak with one voice, and enlightened human reason responds, and confesses both.

LECTURE VI.

AN ARGUMENT FROM THE VISIBLE MARKS OF DESIGN WHICH NATURE REVEALS.

I. *The Ground of the Argument stated.*

1. Designs imply a designer, and contrivances imply a contriver. No argument is necessary, and no proof can be required, to cause men to believe the above statement, which is the major proposition of the argument.

Such is the nature of the human mind, and such the spontaneity of human reason, that no person needs to be told that there can be no design without a designer, and no contrivance without a contriver. Tell any ordinary mind that any given part of a thing is less than the whole, and that all the parts are equal to the whole, or that two things separately equal to a third, are equal to each other, and no proof will be demanded, for the simple reason that the person hearing the statements, knows, intuitively, that they are true, without proof or process of reasoning. So when the intelligence recognizes marks of design anywhere, and in any form, it knows, with equal certainty, that there is, or has been, a designer. Also when the intelligence apprehends what it recognizes as a contrivance, it knows with absolute certainty, that there is or has been a contriver. If a person should see what he was sure was a human foot-print in the sand, he would be equally sure a human foot had been there.

The major proposition, then, is self-evident, a necessary truth, leaving no ground for difference of opinion.

2. The visible universe reveals various marks of design, and is itself, as a whole, and in many of its distinct parts, a contrivance. This is the minor proposition of the argument, and the one that will be disputed, if any, and hence the one which demands proof. If this proposition be admitted, or if it can be proved, it will follow that there is a designer, a contriver, back of, and before Nature, who, in forming Nature, has left the imprint of his intelligence upon its face. This designer and contriver, being before Nature, must be the Eternal One, the God of the Theist.

The first proposition being self-evident, if the second be proved, it will follow by an irresistible conclusion, that there is a God.

II. *The Argument Illustrated and Verified.*

The visible universe carries upon its face very legible marks of design, and is itself a vast contrivance.

The argument need not be pushed into the

immensity of space, in search of the fixed stars, so called ; our own solar system is quite sufficient to give it all the force of which its nature will admit. Nor is it best that the argument should be thoroughly and exclusively astronomical. Such an argument would necessarily be very conclusive with those thoroughly learned in the science ; but would be too vast, and would draw its proofs from facts too far beyond the common circle of human thought, to be appreciated by any save such as have given more than usual attention to sidereal studies. There is a general knowledge of the machinery of the universe, understood and believed by most persons, to which an appeal can be made, as follows :

The child has seen the sun rise and set, has seen the moon wax and wane, and has seen the stars appear and disappear. The child looked upward with emotions of beauty, sublimity and grandeur, which it could not explain, as the shadows of a summer evening gathered around it, and as one star after another came through its fancied canopy of blue, like the lighting up of one candle after another, until the whole heavens became one vast field of bespangled glory. That child then asked, who made all those lights ? and with its little mind burdened with what it had seen, and perhaps burdened still more with the answer it had received in reply to its question, it fell asleep, and on looking out, in the morning, the stars were all gone, and it wondered where so many lights had hid themselves.

It may be said, these are the unscientific wonders of childhood, which riper years, aided by science, will dissipate. They are the unscientific wonders of childhood, and therefore quite limited, obscure, and somewhat vague wonders, which riper years, aided by science, will bring out in more definite form, and in higher and more awful grandeur. At every step of progress in the path of science, from childhood onward to the ripe scholarship of mature years, wonders increase in number and magnitude.

Let the child learn that this earth is round, and that it is suspended in space or hung upon nothing ; and that it rolls round once in twenty-four hours, producing night and day, by rolling us alternately from and to the sun.

Let the child learn that the moon is a smaller body, in form like our earth, and that like our earth it is hung upon nothing and rolls round, and also passes round the earth once in about twenty-eight days, producing all the changes observable in it.

Let the child then learn that this earth, with the moon attending it, performs a journey round the sun once in a little over three hundred and sixty-five days and six hours, or one year: thereby producing all the seasons, Spring, Summer, Autumn and Winter.

Let the child next learn that this earth is one of thirteen worlds, several of which have moons like this, and that they all whirl, and also all travel round the sun like our earth.

Let it also be demonstrated to the child, that these worlds move, in their circuits round the sun, at different distances from it; that the nearest to the sun is thirty-seven millions of miles from it. Also, that this earth moves at a distance of ninety-five millions of miles from the sun, making its yearly journey, five hundred and seventy millions of miles, to accomplish which, it must fly at the rate of more than sixty-five thousand miles per hour.

Let the child now understand that the most distant world from the sun performs a journey round it of sixteen thousand eight hundred millions of miles.

Finally, let the child, or rather the man — for he must be approaching manhood by this time — understand that these thirteen worlds, of which this earth is one, with their moons, move round their center, the sun, as regularly as our sun rises and sets, and our seasons roll round. No clock, *or machine* for measuring time, can be constructed by human skill, which will run so exactly from age to age, as this great clock, whose wheels are mighty worlds. On this state of things, let the following facts be considered:

1. There is, most clearly, an arrangement of worlds in which part is adapted to part, and world is adjusted to, and balanced against world, so as to produce an exact equality of forces and counter-forces, by which all these worlds are propelled and held in their own orbits. This is not accomplished by

material guards, as railroad cars are made to keep the track, but it is done in space, by an unseen influence called attraction and repulsion, which defies human scrutiny.

2. This machinery has run six thousand years, according to the smallest calculation, while many suppose it to be much older, and yet none of its parts have failed; none of its motion has abated; none of its momentum appears exhausted, and no irregularity has attended it. So far as is known, the light and heat of the sun are just as intense as they were a thousand years ago, and the great clock of time has made no approach towards running down, as all man-made clocks do and ever must. While all man-invented lights and heat consume and waste by their own action in lighting and warming surrounding bodies; and all man-contrived forces are exhausted by the action of their own momentum, the sun, and moon, and all the stars, give just as much light as they ever did, and perform their revolutions in the same time they ever did, and all their transits are marked by the same regularity they were a thousand years ago.

3. While the above facts are undeniable, there has been found in nature no power, no efficiency, and no law which could have brought the parts of the great machine together, much less have formed its separate parts, so adapted to each other as to constitute the complex perfect whole. No power or law is found in nature which could restore the

harmony of the machine, if it were thrown out of gearing. If we deny the existence of a Creator, it is not possible to imagine how this machine was formed and got together in such perfection. No known power of nature could have produced it, and no human intellect has yet been able to conceive even a hypothesis how it came to be as it is, which can stand the test of reason for one moment. Men may affirm what they will, concerning their own blindness on the subject, yet it must be impossible for any rational mind to contemplate the machinery of the heavens, and understand its parts, and the relation which part sustains to part, and the adjustment of all its forces, without being conscious of the affirmation of reason within ; that it gives evidence of design, and that the whole is a vast contrivance of a vast intellect.

Having passed, in our investigation, from the unscientific view of childhood to the scientific view of manhood, the averment is proved, which was made, that riper years, aided by Science, would bring out the wonders of the child in more definite forms and more awful grandeur. Wonders, and increasing wonders rise to view at each step in the path of Science, and are seen clearer in each increased degree of scientific light. So great is the wonder which a view of the Universe produces in the rational mind, that reason can relieve itself of the burden, only by taking shelter under the conclusion that there is a God, an Infinite Creator, whose wisdom planned, and whose power built and upholds it.

The argument is now finished, and may be closed by a statement of the propositions of which it is composed:

First. Where designs are seen, there must be a designer; and where contrivance is visible, there must be a contriver.

Second. The visible Universe reveals clear marks of design, and is itself a vast contrivance.

Third. There is, therefore, a designer and contriver, who must have existed before the Universe, and who, by His intelligence, designed and contrived it, and by His power made it what it is. That designer, and contriver, and builder, is God, the Eternal One.

The above argument rests upon a very general view of the material Universe, but there are particular portions, which reveal marks of design, and constitute contrivances in themselves, as parts of the great whole. It will be the object of a few future Lectures, to elaborate arguments from some of these detached portions of God's great work.

LECTURE VII.

THE EXISTENCE OF GOD PROVED FROM THE PHENOMENA OF LIFE.

I. *Ground of the Argument Stated—Life not inherent in Matter.*

1. Life is an undefinable, and inexplicable mystery. If the simple question be asked, what is life? no one can give a direct, clear and descriptive answer. Whence came life at first, and whither does it go, when death transpires? Death, we know, is the absence of life, and to die, we know, is to cease to live; but what is that vital force which we call life, no one can tell. Much of the phenomena of life, and much of the action of the vital force, in the process of living, may be known and described, but the life itself remains unknown, the most profound mystery to him who liveth.

2. One of the facts which may be known, in regard to life is, that it is not inherent in matter, and is no essential part or quality of matter. It is upon this fact that the present argument rests.

3. Life not being an essential property of matter, yet existing in connection with matter, and in such a manner that matter lives, or is alive, it follows

that life must be imparted to matter by a higher power ; and if there be a higher power than matter, and all the life of matter, a power that has produced life, and imparted it to matter, that power must be God, and Atheism is overthrown.

That life is not an essential property of matter, if not self-evident, becomes manifest upon the slightest observation. If life were an essential property of matter, all matter would be alive, nor could there be any such thing as death, or absence of life. We know this is not the case, for we see live matter and dead matter, and all living matter dies around us. Life, then, is not an essential element of matter, but is imparted to it whenever matter passes life.

4. The only possible resort of Atheism, at this stage of the argument, to save itself from annihilation, is to affirm that life is the result of organization. This ground is often taken, and in proof, the fact is urged, that life is found only in connection with organized matter. It is admitted that life is developed only in connection with certain organizations ; but this does not relieve the difficulty in the slightest degree, but rather increases it, as will be made to appear.

II. *The Main Point Proved—Life is not the result of organization.*

1. No known combination of material elements will produce either animal or vegetable life. A

plant may be analyzed, and all the parts of matter it contains, and the proportion of each, can be ascertained, and yet no human skill can put them together so as to produce life, and thus originate a living plant.

In like manner, an animal body can be analyzed, and all the parts and properties can be ascertained. All the organs of life can be examined, and their functions pointed out, and yet the vital force, the life, is something different from any or all of these. These organs may all remain entire and intact, after life has left the material organism. Chemistry can take the animal economy to pieces, and tell just what and how many material elements compose it, and in what proportion the parts are combined, yet no known power can impart vitality to these combined elements ; life must have a higher origin.

2. Life precedes organization, and therefore cannot be the result of organization. So far is life from being the result of the organization of matter, that it is clearly the power that produces the organization. When Atheists affirm that life is the result of organization, they subvert the law of being, by putting the cause for the effect, and the effect for the cause. Life is the cause of organization, and hence, the organization cannot account for the life, but the life accounts for the organization. To make the organization account for life, is to make an effect account for the existence of its own cause, which is an absurdity. Life, therefore, can be

accounted for only by supposing a higher power, acting back of both organization and life, and that higher power must be God.

The organization of the material elements of both vegetable and animal bodies, commences in an embryo state, around its nucleus, life ; life is the first thing that acts, and it begins the process, and is the vital and vitalizing power of assimilation, which gathers to itself the appropriate material elements, and completes the organization. It is clear that life precedes the organization, and therefore cannot be produced by it. It is equally clear that life, residing in the organization which it has assimilated to itself, by the same vitalizing and assimilating power, repairs its waste, and counteracts the tendency of all organized matter to decomposition, until, having accomplished its mission, it withdraws and lets the organization return to its primitive elements.

It may now be regarded as settled, that life is not an essential, inhering property of matter, and is not the result of the organization of matter, and hence it must be conditioned upon some power distinct from and above matter, and if so, Atheism must be false, and Theism must be true.

III. *The conclusion reached above, verified by another class of arguments.*

1. Life of every kind is derived, transmitted, and perpetuated by a succession of individual lives, each

life in the chain of succession being distinct, one and indivisible. Life is not one whole identical life, but the whole is composed of a succession of lives, each constituting a distinct, whole, perfect life, by itself. Every life, of every kind, is derived from a prior life of its own kind. This succession of lives is proof positive that there must have been a first life of each kind, which was not derived from a prior life, as all subsequent lives have been derived, but which must have been the result of a pre-existing life-giving power, and that power is God the Creator.

The Atheist will look in vain for a subterfuge that will evade the above conclusion, in the oft-repeated affirmation, that life is the result of nature's own spontaneity. Such an affirmation is an assumption which is not, and cannot be sustained by any kind or degree of evidence ; while, on the other hand, the well known operations of nature contradict it. There are two facts which must overwhelm this assumption of the Atheist.

(1.) No power or operative force of nature has yet been discovered which can originate life ; nature's only power being to transmit it, when and where it already exists.

(2.) Nature has never been known to produce life, but only to foster and develop it, where, in some form, it had been deposited. Nature has never been known to produce or develop life, without a seed, a germ, a scion, or root, which contained the vital principle of life. Under no circumstance has nature been known to originate life, or develop it, without the deposition of a germ, in some form. If nature had ever been known to bring forth life of any kind, and in any form, without a seed or germ, Atheists would point to such facts with an air of triumph, but in this nature responds not to their views. Earth, air and water combined in any possible proportions, aided by the summer sun, has no power to develop life, until the vital element has been supplied, and the conclusion is, that there is no inherent power in nature that can originate life.

2. The different kinds and forms of life which nature develops are distinct, the one from the other, and never cross or blend. The Atheist, on being driven by the preceding argument from his position, that life is the result of nature's own spontaneity, may attempt another subterfuge, by affirming that while nature is never known to develop life, at once, in its higher forms, the result is reached by its own law and force of progress. The proposition stated above overthrows this position. Nature has never developed any such law and force of progress. One uniform law governs all the operations of nature in her developments of life ; like produces like. Nature, in the transmission of life, in every case, transmits the kind of life she receives in the germ deposited with her, preserving each succession of lives distinct, the one from the other. Climate and culture may modify, but cannot originate what did not exist in

kind in the parent. Here nature is true to her trust; she never receives the germ of one kind of life and responds by developing another kind of life. She never receives the seeds of the herbaceous plant, and develops the woody shrub or tree. She never receives the filbert and develops the oak. She never receives the acorn and develops the pine. So she never receives the deposit of vegetable life of any kind, and in response, throws out animal life, even of the lowest grade. Under her care, vegetable life never progresses into animal life. And so with every kind of animal life, she preserves each distinct. Under her care, no kind of life progresses beyond its own nature, to be lost in another and a higher kind. There is no progress from one kind of life to another. Under nature's faithful charge, every kind of life sends forth its own stream, like itself, and each branch of life runs on its own rounds of succession, without crossing or intermingling with other successions of life. Herbs never progress into trees, vegetable life never progresses into animal life, and one kind of animal life never progresses into another and higher kind of animal life. Oysters never become fish with fins; reptiles never rise above reptiles; fishes never become bipeds, or quadrupeds, and never drop their fins and scales, and don feathers and wings, and become fowls of heaven; and brutes never progress into men.

If the Atheist could produce one clear case of a deviation from these laws, he would pretend, at least, to consider his cause gained, but he finds not one fact in all the realm of nature. Suppose it had been known, no matter how long ago, that pine trees grew from acorns, that apple trees grew from filberts, that petted toads feathered out and became hens and ducks; that children had been known to grow as fruit upon some plants or trees, and to drop off like ripe fruit, in full developed infancy; or suppose oysters had been known to become fish without shells, and with fins and scales; and fish had been known to turn into mermaids, and mermaids had improved into real human beings; and suppose all this had clearly resulted from nature's own progressive force, the Atheist would give a shout of triumph over the revelation of such facts. But there is no such illustration found amid all the operations of nature. Nature has never been known to develop life, without first receiving the deposit of the vital principle, in each case, and then she has only developed the kind of life, the vital power of which she received. This all proves that the first life, of each kind, must have had an origin, distinct from, and above nature, and to account for that we must fall back upon the Theistic belief in the existence of God.

IV. *The Argument summed up and concluded.*

1. The following points have been proved:

(1.) Life is not inherent in matter, as one of its essential qualities, but is something added to it whenever matter is vitalized, or may be said to live, or to be alive.

(2) Life is not the result of organization. The organization of matter does not originate life, but the presence, vitalizing and assimilating power of life, originates the organization.

(3.) Life, of each kind, exists, not as one whole, but in a succession of individual lives, each a distinct identity, and indivisible.

(4.) There is no known power in nature which can originate life, only as the medium of transmission from a pre-existing life ; and nature never has been known to develop life, without the deposition of a germ in some form.

(5.) Life is not developed by any force or law of progress in nature, by which the lower forms of life are improved into the higher, but each kind and form is preserved distinct, and maintains its identity from age to age.

2. From the above facts in regard to life, which have been established beyond a doubt, the conclusion follows irresistibly, that life, in each of its distinct forms, had a beginning. There must have been a first life of each kind. To say that life had no beginning, in view of the above facts, is to outrage one's own common sense. We never saw or heard of vegetable, or animal life, that had no beginning ; and from the points proved, or from what is seen and known of life, reason makes the undeniable deduction, that every plant, and every tree, and

every animal, and every human being, that ever lived, began to live, and that, therefore, there was a beginning of the first life of each kind. No matter how far you carry your reasoning backward along the chain of successive lives, with the facts proved before the mind, it is not possible, at any remote period in the past, to think of the life of a plant, tree, animal or man, that had no beginning. Finitude, or a beginning, and end, is so impressed upon each life, in all visible successions of life, that he who pretends to believe that once there lived a plant, tree, animal or man, whose life had no beginning, does violence to his own reason.

3. The fact now established, that life had a beginning, entirely overthrows Atheism, and establishes Theism. Atheism does not and cannot account for that beginning of life which has been proved. Indeed, Atheism can account for nothing, for its fundamental principle, that there is no God, no Creator, precludes the possibility of a beginning to any thing, as it precludes all cause for any thing, and renders everything necessarily eternal, which the eyes of the Atheist must tell him is false. He sees things beginning and ending, living and dying, all around him every day, and yet in his madness adopts a theory which implies that there is no first cause for anything. It is, then, impossible for an Atheist to account for the beginning of life, which has been proved; and yet, to deny a beginning is to affirm that there exists a series of lives, perpet-

ually increasing in number, which had no beginning, which is to affirm a mathematical impossibility. On the other hand, for the Atheist to admit that life had a beginning, is to admit that there was a cause for that beginning, and that cause must have existed prior to the beginning of all successions of life, and hence, could itself have had no cause, and must have been eternal and creative, and of course, is the God of the Theist. Thus is it not only proved that there is a God, but the idea of God is rendered universal, and is revealed as a necessary idea of reason, in the presence of the five facts which have been established, concerning life. The idea that there is a God, a Creator, cannot be escaped without affirming that life commenced without a cause, or that nothing produced it, or that a limited and increasing series of lives had no beginning ; each and all of which is impossible ; and as neither of these can be true, the other only possible thing must be true — there is a God, the author and source of life.

A word only is necessary to show that the Scriptures teach, on this subject, in harmony with the voice of nature. Israel's ancient bard, in his song to the God of the Bible, sang, "With THEE is the fountain of life."

LECTURE VIII.

THE EXISTENCE OF GOD PROVED FROM THE EXISTENCE OF THE HUMAN FAMILY.

The following argument rests upon the fact that physical humanity cannot be rationally accounted for, only upon the hypothesis that there is a God who created a first man and a first woman, from whom all other human beings have descended by natural generation.

The plan of the argument is to state all the conceivable methods of accounting for the existence of humanity, as it is, and then to prove that they are all impossible, or false, except the Theistic one, stated above. If the premises are made sufficiently broad, to comprehend all conceivable methods of accounting for the existence of our race, and the reasoning on each point be clear and conclusive, the argument will be demonstrative.

There are but four conceivable methods of accounting for the existence of the human family, three of which have sometimes been resorted to by Atheists, and the fourth is the Theistic mode, by supposing a Creator, God. These four methods shall now be examined.

I. *The Theory of Eternal Generation.*

This assumes that the human race had no beginning, and, of course, that there never was a first man and a first woman, and that the race is eternal.

In opposition to this theory, it is affirmed that it is impossible, a contradiction upon its face, and that there must have been a first man and first woman, who did descend from a previously existing man and woman. In support of this denial of the assumption of eternal generation, the following considerations are urged :

1. It was proved in Lecture III, that time, and all that is evolved in and by time, had a beginning, which is comprehensive of the race of human beings ; it must, therefore, have had a beginning.

2. It was proved in Lecture V, from the developments of Geology, that the human family is more recent than the earth, vegetables and animals, human remains being found only on or near the surface of the earth.

3. It was proved in the last Lecture that life had a beginning, which is comprehensive of the position that the race of human beings had a beginning. It was shown that life is not one whole, but a succession of individual lives, and that succession necessarily involves a beginning.

4. Humanity is known to us only as possessing a limited existence, with a beginning and an end, pertaining to each individual of the race. Every indi-

vidual known to us, personally or by history, began to be, and has ceased or must cease to be. Now, what is true of all the individuals, must be true of the race composed of such individuals. In the light of these facts, it is impossible to conceive of the race as having had no beginning. To suppose a race of beings without a beginning, composed of individuals, every one of which has a beginning and an end, is simply to suppose an impossibility.

5. It is impossible to conceive of our race as having had no beginning, without conceiving of, at least, one man and one woman which had no beginning. This must be more difficult of conception, and harder to believe, than the Theistic idea of a Creator.

But to suppose a man and woman once existed, who had no beginning, is to suppose that they were eternal, and consequently self-existent. If they were self-existent, they had no cause of existence, only what was in themselves, and that must have been an eternal cause; and hence, it must have ever remained a cause; and the conclusion is undeniable, that the eternal father and mother of our race must be alive somewhere upon the earth. Such eternal self-existent persons could not die, since the only cause of their existence is an eternal cause, and in themselves. And if there be no God to take them away, they must now be living upon the earth. Would it not be worth a search, to find and look upon the venerable pair who never began to be, and to hear, in their own words, the history of their immortal round of life in the midst of this world of their dying children.

The argument need be pushed no farther,—reason repudiates such a hypothesis,—as a method of accounting for the origin of our race. It is impossible to believe it; it must, therefore, be dismissed as absurd and false.

II. *The Progressive Theory.*

This theory assumes that there is in nature a progressive force, by which the higher and more perfect forms of being have been developed from lower forms by the action of nature's own law of progress. According to this theory, humanity had its origin in the oyster, or some other half-animal, half-vegetable existence, and that half-animal, half-vegetable something, was developed from vegetable life, and that again sprang by the force of nature from inorganic matter.

In reply to this theory, the following considerations are offered:

1. If all were allowed that is claimed for nature's progressive law, it would not account for the origin of our race, but only throw the first cause further back, leaving it unexplained. If man sprang from an oyster, the question arises,—from whence came the oyster? There must be just as much difficulty in accounting for the race of oysters, as for the race of men. If it be said the oyster sprang from inor-

ganic matter, two questions arise, which the theory leaves unanswered:

(1.) Where did the matter come from?

(2.) What was the cause of the change in matter, from an inorganic to an organic state, from an inanimate to an animate state?

The theory furnishes no answer to these questions. If it were assumed that the matter was eternal, the assumption would imply that a first change from an inorganic to an organic state would be impossible, because it could have no cause.

2. There is no such law of progress in nature. This is an assumption, not only without proof, but in the face of positive proof. Nature has never revealed the slightest sign of such a law of progress, not one fact has ever occurred to suggest its existence. On the other hand, nature has ever been uniform in her operations, acting under one undeviating law of conservatism, by which every thing is preserved in its own identity and nature, and held in its own rounds of succession, like descending from like.

3. This theory has been exploded and entirely overthrown in preceding Lectures:

(1.) In Lecture III. it was proved that the present form of the material universe had a beginning. While that argument was elaborated in view of time, as measured by the revolutions of the heavenly bodies, the principle is comprehensive of the present argument, as it most clearly involves a beginning to every form that nature wears, and a cause for such beginning. Nature, in the form of humanity, must have had a beginning; even if it be by progress, it must have had a beginning, and a cause for that beginning of progress.

(2.) In Lecture IV. and V, it was proved that matter is not eternal, but that it was created and had a beginning, which entirely overthrows the progressive theory. If matter was first created, nothing is gained by the progressive theory, since the existence of a Creator is then proved, which will equally account for the existence of man.

(3.) It was proved in Lecture VII, that animal life had a beginning, in which argument the progressive theory was directly met and overthrown. What was there proved of the life of men, must be equally true of the material organism in which that life inheres. These arguments need not be repeated; this reference to them as applicable to the progressive theory is sufficient, and it stands distinctly and conclusively overthrown.

III. *The Accidental Theory.*

This theory supposes the first of the race to have happened by chance; that, without the action of intelligence, the fortuitous coming together of the required parts of matter, produced a man. This may be regarded as the Atheist's last resort, and hence, if he be overthrown here, his defeat is complete and final. Let us, then, test this last and strong hold of Atheistic Infidelity. It must have required a combination of concurrent accidents to produce the race of humanity in this way, too numerous and vast to admit of belief. The following outline presents but a part of what must be required.

1. The frame-work of the human body consists of about two hundred and fifty bones. These are all so framed together as to make a perfect whole. And so perfect is the whole, that the following statements are true, beyond doubt:

(1.) The frame is so complete that no bone could be added which would improve it.

(2.) No bone could be removed which would not impair it.

(3.) No bone could be altered without damage, so perfectly are all the bones fitted together.

(4.) No two bones could change places without damage to the frame, so perfect is the whole arrangement, and so exactly are all the bones fitted to each other, and each fitted for its own place.

2. The bones are all framed together in such a manner, and the joints so constructed, as to give the greatest strength where most strength is needed; as to favor rapid motion where quick motion is most needed; and slow motion where slow motion is most needed; and so as to retard or prevent motion where easy and free motion would impair and weaken the structure. The particulars of what has been stated might be pointed out, but it is unnecessary, the facts are so obvious. Such is the frame-work

of the human body, and if the argument was left here it would be conclusive, for it is impossible to suppose that it could come into existence without an intelligent, designing cause. There are so many adaptations, presenting such a combination of contrivances, as to set skepticism at defiance. Two hundred and fifty bones, most of which present two distinct adaptations, each end being adapted to its fellow-bone. Then each of these adaptations involves another adaptation, being adapted to perform a given motion, and to perform it by means which will, at the same time, prevent other motions, which would interfere with the general design of the structure. Can reason conceive all this possible without an intelligent author? Never; and he who affirms it, affirms without consideration, or falsifies his own convictions. But, as yet, we have only the opening of the argument before us, and will proceed.

3. The bones, above noticed, are all tied together in a manner which proves it to be the work of intelligence. They are not all fastened together in the same way.

(1.) Where little or no motion is required, they are fastened more firmly, as though they were framed and pinned together.

(2.) Where limited motion is required, they are united by cartilage, sometimes called gristle.

(3.) Where extended and easy motion is required, they are united by ligaments, which are less confining and allow of ready and free play.

(4.) All the joints, where two bones are united, are lubricated or oiled with a very slippery fluid, called sinavia. The secretion of this fluid is provided for in the joint, which is no less an evidence of design, and no less a contrivance, than the oil can, always kept at hand by him who runs a machine.

4. The frame being completed, the whole is securely covered with a peculiar membrane, called the periosteum. This answers a two-fold purpose.

(1.) It nourishes the bones by means of the vessels which pass through it for that purpose.

(2.) It serves as a ground upon which the muscles and tendons are set. It being firmly attached to the bones, and the muscles and tendons being firmly attached to it, it holds them from breaking loose by their powerful action.

5. The bones are filled with an oily substance called marrow, upon which their life, health and strength, appear to depend.

6. The frame being finished, there must be added the locomotion power, for the bones are only levers, and can act only as they are acted upon. To effect this, the whole is filled out with flesh and handsomely covered with skin, which adds form and beauty to the whole. The flesh constitutes the muscles which move the bones. The large and full muscles taper off at each extremity into a cordy, powerful substance, called tendons, which are firmly attached to the bones. By the contraction and relaxation of the muscles, the bones are moved,

and the machine is started and made to operate. But the muscles are not self-moving, but act only as the ropes and belts of a machine, which connect the working parts with the working power. There is another power that acts upon them.

7. The nerves are a most wonderful contrivance. They appear like fine, white cords or threads, and when traced to their source, are found to issue from the brain, and from its elongation, called the spinal marrow. The trunks of the nerves are divided and subdivided, until, in their most minute forms, they reach every part of every extremity. There are two classes or sets of nerves.

(1.) One class of these nerves gives the power of sensation, which renders us capable of feeling. They are, hence, called nerves of sensation.

(2.) The other class of nerves gives the power of motion, and are called the voluntary nerves, or nerves of motion. They act upon the muscles at the bidding of the will, and cause them to contract and relax, by which the bones move and the whole machine is made to operate.

8. The human machine, as described above, is further provided with a reproductive apparatus, by which its wastes are supplied, but for which it would soon fail. This department is too multifarious to be described, in detail, in this argument. A mere outline will answer every purpose, so far as the force of the argument is concerned.

(1.) The stomach, which first receives the food

we eat, is a wonderful apparatus, with its appendages. It has the power of reducing what it receives to a common substance, and of assimilating it to the various parts of the organism, adding bone to bone, flesh to flesh, substance to like substance, in every part of the body.

(2.) The blood is a principal agent in this reproductive process. It is formed, principally, from what is eaten, but, in part, from the air that is breathed. To effect the repairing of the system by means of the blood, it is sent coursing through every part in vessels called arteries, and is returned to its starting point in another class of vessels called veins.

(3.) The blood is propelled through its course by the powerful action of the heart, an organ exactly contrived for that purpose.

(4.) Along the course of the blood there are numberless absorbing vessels which take up from the blood, as it passes, the substance which every part of the body requires. Each of these vessels takes up just that material from the blood which the part demands for which it acts, and rejects all the rest. The blood being thus robbed of its vital qualities, it is returned to be renewed for another round. The blood is renewed from two sources, as has been intimated, namely: from the material prepared by the stomach from the food that has been eaten, and from the air that is breathed.

(5.) To effect the renewal of the blood by means of the atmosphere, a breathing apparatus has been prepared. The lungs constitute the most important organ of the breathing machine. The lungs are so constructed as to admit a large quantity of air, and by their action they receive and expel it constantly, from the beginning to the end of life. The blood returning exhausted is passed through the lungs, and thereby brought in contact with the air that is breathed, and absorbs the oxygen of the air, by which it is vitalized and changed from a dark to a light red. The air is exhaled, minus its oxygen, and fresh air is again inhaled, and so the process goes on until death takes place. In this breathing machine the lungs and the air are adapted to each other, and the air and the blood are adapted to each other. If the lungs were not so constructed as to receive the air, give off its oxygen to the blood and expel the remainder, breathing would be impossible or useless. If the air was not composed, as it is, of twenty-one parts of oxygen and seventy-nine parts of nitrogen, it would not subserve the purposes of animal life, and the lungs would be useless, or would inhale death. If the air was differently compounded, it would be a fatal poison.

The wonderful system of reproduction, with its numerous organs, may be summed up under three heads or divisions:

The first is the Laboratory, by which elements are prepared for the support of the system.

The second division embraces the absorption apparatus, by which the prepared elements are taken up and made a part of the organism.

The third is the discharging system, by which all unnecessary matter is thrown off, and thereby the overloading of the system is prevented. This relates not only to the rejected portions of what is eaten, but also to the worn-out parts of the body itself, which has to be re-placed with new matter.

9. The human system is also supplied with a sensation machine, which is no less wonderful, and no less reveals a design. The nerves of sensation were named while treating of the locomotive power, but they must now be looked at as the ground-work of the sensation apparatus. These nerves, which have their seat in the brain, and which terminate in the several local organs of sense, constitute a wonderful machine for seeing, hearing, feeling, tasting and smelling. It will be sufficient to name the visual apparatus. Vision is the result of the wonderful eye, and the wonderful light, and their wonderful adaptation to each other.

The eye is a wonderful thing, in itself. It is too complicated to admit of a minute description in a Lecture like this, without occupying too much time.

(1.) There is a collection of different kinds of matter, the right kinds of matter, the right quantity of matter, and the right proportionate quantity of each kind.

(2.) There is, next, the form of the eye, which constitutes its adaptation to receive the light in the right quantity, and to produce the figure and color of the object emitting or reflecting that light upon the retina.

(3.) Then there is the relation which the two eyes sustain to each other, being so placed as to give the right angle to bring the light that enters each eye to a focus at the right point, so that one act of vision is the result of the action of both eyes, and that vision is rendered stronger by the united action of the two eyes in the act of seeing.

(4.) Finally, we have the place in the body which the eyes occupy. There is no other place in the body where they could be set with the same advantage. They are set high up in the structure, so as to place them out of the way of the more active portions of the frame, and out of the way of the material objects upon which we expend our greatest physical exertion. They are set in front, as it is more necessary to see where we are going than to see where we have been, and yet so as to enable us to see on either side if there be a better way than a strait line before us.

The eye, then, as an apparatus for seeing, is too wonderful to be the result of anything less than a master intellect acting from design, carrying out the ideal which existed in the intelligence before an eye was formed of matter. A *camera obscura* is an apparatus which represents the eye. The images of external objects are received through a double convex glass, and are exhibited in their native colors on some white surface placed within the machine, in the focus of the glass. This illustrates the philosophy of vision, so far as the structure of the eye and the action of light are concerned.

To suppose that this camera obscura was not designed, and contrived, and adapted to the light, by intelligence; to suppose that it was formed by crystalization, or that it grew as a fruit, or that it came into being without any previously existing cause, would be less absurd than to suppose that the first pair of eyes grew in the head of the first man without the action of intelligence. But suppose this great accident did occur, that the first two eyes were a mere accident, still a greater accident must be supposed, which is, that the first two eyes happened to select their location in the head and not elsewhere, happened to get in such relation to each other, and in so happening, without design or intelligence, they happened to produce a universal and unvarying law, by which all eyes have followed their example in selecting for themselves the same position in the body. To believe all this, must require a much larger degree of credulity than is required to believe that there is a God who formed the eye.

(5.) But the eye itself does not give us vision without light. The wonderful eye would have happened in vain, if there had happened to be no light, or if light had happened to be unsuited to the eye. Light, we know, is adapted to the eye, as the medium of vision. It is a wonderful element, but little understood. White light is said to be a compound of seven different colors, yet in its purity it is invisible, while it renders everything else visible upon which it falls. Did light happen to be, and to be just what it is? If so, by what a profound accident did this world escape the fate of unbroken darkness, though full of accidental eyes.

In the above outline of physical humanity, only a part of its wonderful machinery has been revealed; it is proper, therefore, to make a comprehensive statement of what cannot be given in detail.

10. The human organism, as a compound whole, is composed of more than ten thousand parts, the want of any one of which would impair, if not ruin the whole machine. It must have been a tremendous accident that produced so many adaptations, so many concurrent facts in so small a compass. The existence of one human body, as it is, involves more than ten thousand adaptations of part to part, within itself, besides the adaptation of the whole to an end, and its adaptations to external surroundings, as the lungs to the air, the eyes to the light, and the ear to the atmosphere, to produce hearing.

11. But this number of concurrent facts must be doubled, to give existence to the race. There must have been two human beings, one man and one woman, if no more, to originate the race, the human family. There must have been two such tremendous accidents as has been described, each involving more than ten thousand coincident facts, a failure

of any one of which, out of the more than twenty thousand, would have defeated the present result.

12. In the concurrence of the two tremendous accidents, another must have occurred, which is, that one, by accident, was a man, and the other, by accident, was a woman. But for these accidents, there would have been no race of human beings.

13. Still another accident must have occurred, which is, that by accident, the two accidents happened so near together, in point of time, that they both lived at the same time. But for this accident, which made them cotemporary, there would have been no race, even had this wonderful and powerful agent, called accident, produced a thousand men, and as many more women, so remote from each other as not to live at the same time.

14. There must have been yet another accident, which is, that by accident, it happened that the two accidents happened to occur at or so near the same place on this wide earth that the accidental man and the accidental woman accidentally found each other. But for this last named accident, all the other accidents might have occurred a thousand times in portions of the earth remote from each other, without giving existence to the race of mankind.

15. One more most profound accident must have occurred, to make out the case, which is: all these numerous and great accidents must have occurred so as to place themselves and their immediate and remote results, under a fixed law, by the action of

which the race has ever since been developed and perpetuated ; so that since those first great accidents, nothing in this matter has been left to, or occurred by accident. If the history of humanity recorded, now and then, a like accident ; and if one or two had undoubtedly occurred in our own times, it would greatly strengthen the faith of those who believe that the original production of humanity was an accident ; but such accidents have never been repeated. As impossible as it is to believe all this, it must be believed, and much more of the same kind, if the existence of God, the Creator, be denied.

The argument need be pushed no further. Reason repudiates the supposition of such an origin of humanity, as absurd, and a thousand times more unreasonable than the Theistic belief in the existence of God, who created all things.

IV. *The Theistic Theory is the only remaining one.*

The Theist affirms that there is a God, who created a first man, and a first woman, from whom all other human beings have derived their existence by natural generation.

It has been shown that there are but four methods of accounting for the existence of the human race, of which this last named is one. The three former have been proved to be absurd, false, and impossible ; and the conclusion is irresistible, that the fourth and last named must be true ; there is, therefore, a God, a Creator.

LECTURE IX.

AN ARGUMENT FOUNDED UPON THE PHENOMENA OF THE HUMAN MIND.

PRELIMINARY REMARKS.

We now enter a field of investigation different from those that have been occupied in gathering the facts which have constituted the basis of preceding arguments. Arguments have been drawn from matter, in several of its forms and relations, and notwithstanding it is destitute of intelligence, it has been found to bear visible marks of intelligence impressed upon it; seen in its arrangements, adaptations, and in the contrivances into which it has been formed by some unseen contriving, arranging and organizing force.

In now turning to the investigation of mind, we have a very different element to deal with, as mind is not matter, and is not governed by the laws that govern matter. Mind differs from matter as widely as thought does from the marble pillar. The law which governs mind differs from the law which governs matter as widely as the argument or motive that sways the mind differs from the power of the rock, which crushes by its weight. The law which brings the loosened rock bounding down the mountain side cannot be confounded with the law that carries the man up the same mountain side, for the sake of the prospect its lofty summit will afford.

The power to think, feel, and will are the most wonderful of all powers, and lie so far beyond the comprehension of the thinking mind itself, as to awaken thoughts of a Higher Power, as the author and source of intelligence.

It is not proposed to give a detailed analysis of mental phenomena, for the purpose of developing the evidence it might thus be made to contribute towards proving the existence of God ; a few leading facts only will be presented, which will render the argument more simple, without materially diminishing its force.

The argument will be made to depend, mainly, upon two facts, both fundamental in their nature.

1. Intelligence is not matter, is no quality of matter, and matter is not intelligent.

2. While intelligence is not matter, and matter is not intelligent, the two are so fitted to each other, and so united in the human organism, as jointly to constitute an intellectual machine, for knowing the material world.

I. *Intelligence is not matter, is no quality of matter, and matter is not intelligent.*

The thinking and knowing power in man, is

spirit, and not matter. We call it spirit, soul, or mind, but whatever we call it, it is distinguished from the body, and hence it is not matter, not material, but immaterial. This is a vital principle, and if it can be established on natural and philosophical grounds, it will go far towards establishing the existence of God as the Creator "of the spirits of all flesh." So far as is known, all who admit the immateriality, spirituality, and immortality of the human soul or mind, also admit the existence of God.

The bearing which this point has upon the question of the existence of God will be shown after the fact in regard to the mind has been established.

It is a significant fact, that the distinction between body and soul, matter and mind, is a universal idea. All men, in all ages, and in all lands, have recognized a distinction between the body and mind. Men have never been in the habit of confounding the body with the knowing power which resides in the body. While the idea of a distinction between body and mind is nearly or quite universal, existing as commonly among the ignorant and unlettered as among the learned, philosophy has reduced that distinction to a scientific certainty, by noting the phenomena of each as so diverse as not to be given by the same element.

We are now in a field of investigation where we are required to reason from natural principles, and this we can do only so far as science lights our path, and we can reason only in the light of science as it now shines, taking its clearest aspects, and using all the light we have, until we can develop more. What, then, does philosophy teach?

Philosophy teaches us that all we know of matter or mind, is the phenomena they give us ; and hence, it teaches us, where we find two classes of phenomena, which are of such opposite natures as not to be given by the same substance, we know there must be two elements. On this principle, philosophy draws a line between matter and mind. Mind is that which perceives, thinks, knows, wills, feels, loves, hates, and is joyful and sorrowful. Matter is that which gives the phenomena of impenetrability, inertia, extension, divisibility, figure, color, &c. These two classes of phenomena cannot inhere in the same substance, and hence, matter and mind cannot be the same thing. To deny the distinction between them is to set ourselves against, not only the universal opinion of the unlearned world, but against the world's philosophy, as held and taught by the most learned and wise. A few illustrations of the principle involved will be sufficient on this point.

1. The phenomena of volition cannot be given by the same substance that gives the phenomena of inertia. Volition, which is a mental power, is the power of self-action ; but inertia, which is a quality of matter, is the absence of the power of self-action ; it being capable of acting only as it is acted upon.

It is therefore certain that mind and matter are not the same thing.

2. The phenomena of intelligence cannot be given by the same element that gives the phenomena of extension, divisibility, figure, color, and inertia. The power to know is and must be self-acting, and of that which is self-acting, not one of the qualities of matter can be affirmed. The power to know must be a simple and indivisible power, and therefore cannot inhere in matter, which is divisible.

No one can contend that matter is intelligent, unless upon one of two assumptions, neither of which can be true.

(1.) The assumption that intelligence is an essential property of matter, cannot be sustained. If it were so, every part and particle of matter would be intelligent, and whatever is not intelligent, if any such thing there be, cannot be matter. That which is destitute of any essential property of matter cannot be matter. All matter is not intelligent, does not think, know and feel, and therefore intelligence is not an essential property of matter.

(2.) The assumption that matter, not embracing intelligence as one of its essential properties, becomes intelligent by having intelligence superadded to it, cannot be maintained on Atheistic ground. If there be no God, matter must be eternal, and if intelligence is not an essential property of matter, nothing but matter originally existed, and there being no God, there could be no intelligence to add to mat-

5

ter, and no power to add it. Therefore, upon the Atheistic theory, matter could never become intelligent by having intelligence superadded to it.

Matter could not add intelligence to itself. The idea that matter added intelligence to itself, must suppose that intelligence existed outside of and separate from matter, which overthrows the whole theory of the intelligence of matter.

It is equally impossible that matter should originate intelligence within and of itself. As it is now admitted that matter does not possess intelligence, as an essential quality, it must be something beside matter, and distinct from matter; and to say that matter originates it, is to say that matter creates a new thing, which did not before exist, and that this new thing is created out of nothing, for it could not create it out of itself. To suppose that matter created intelligence out of itself, would be to suppose that it so changed itself as to cease to be matter. To suppose that matter, as an active power, or cause, should use itself up in producing intelligence, another and distinct entity, is not only philosophically impossible, but if allowed, would prove, after all, that it is not matter, but something else, that is intelligent.

It is, then, certain that intelligence is not an essential property of matter, and that it is not and cannot be something superadded to matter. The conclusion is undeniable, that intelligence is not matter, and that matter is not intelligent.

3. The phenomena of memory proves that the mind, which remembers, is not matter, and is no part of what is called the body. Take as an illustration, a single mind, possessing the largest amount of knowledge, and there is no known philosophy which will explain how such a vast storehouse of ideas can exist in man, upon the assumption that the mind is matter. Thoughts, ideas, knowledge, and volitions are immaterial. The objects of knowledge may be material, but the knowledge of the object is immaterial. I behold a mountain, it is a material object impressed upon my sense through the medium of vision, but the mountain is not in my eye, and is not, in substance, in or on my brain. I close my eyes, or turn away from seeing the mountain, and think of it, and it is not now, in substance, in my mind. There is only a thought, or notion of it, in the mind, embracing its size, form, &c. I saw it and it was then in my mind only in thought ; I now remember it and it is not in my mind, I have only a conception of it. I may have seen a hundred mountains, and remember them all ; I may have become learned in all the sciences, and remember their varied principles and their applications ; I may have studied the history of all nations, and be capable of remembering the origin and principal events attending each ; and in addition to all this, I can remember my own history, embracing most of the incidents that have occurred during my life-journey of sixty years. Where are all these

matters stored in the mind, to be called up as occasion requires, upon the assumption that the mind is matter, or that it is the body, or any part of the body? If the whole body was impressed with them, it would not suffice, much less the small space of the brain. The old philosophy of memory, which made it depend upon images stored away, to be brought out in the act of remembering, like the sliding pictures of a panorama, was very unphilosophical. To make the mind material, and then store it with images or pictures of all the sights and thoughts of half a century, is physically and philosophically impossible. But suppose the mind to be spirit, without figure, color, extension, or divisibility, and that the act of remembering is simply the act of the mind in returning to one of its former states, and every absurdity vanishes.

4. The phenomena of conscious identity proves that the mind is no part of the body, and that it is not matter.

The man of sixty years does not believe, but knows that he is the same person that was the child of six years, the youth of sixteen, and the man of thirty; and he knows that it was he, and not another, that performed such acts, and had such an experience along the way as he remembers of himself. If there is not in man a mind, which is not matter, a soul, which is no part of the body, this affirmation of consciousness would be a greater falsehood than tongue ever told. It is not true of the matter that composes the body. The body includes organs for reception and discharge, and the process of waste and renewal is perpetually going on, so that the man of sixty years does not consist of the same matter that constituted the youth of sixteen.

5. The phenomena of conscience proves that the mind is no part of the body, and that it is not matter.

By conscience, here, is meant that sense of self-approbation which we feel when we do what we believe to be right ; and that sense of self-condemnation which we feel when we do what we believe to be wrong. The simple question is, upon what do these judgments of conscience rest ? What is it that feels self-approval or self-condemnation ? It is not the body, not any part of the body. Did any man's feet ever feel guilty for carrying him astray ? or did any man ever blame his feet for not keeping the right road ? Did any man ever feel guilt in his hands for the unlawful acts they performed ? Did any one ever believe his brains were guilty for his evil thoughts, desires, and purposes ? Did any one ever feel his tongue throb with guilt after uttering falsehood to men, or blasphemy against God ? Every one knows that no part of his body bears the guilt of wrong-doing ; guilt rests upon the inner man, the mind, the conscious soul. The argument triumphs over all caviling and all sophistry ; it is what every one knows of himself, it is the voice of the soul, saying, "it is not the body, not the hands or the feet, but I, the soul, I did it, I am the responsible agent, I am the guilty one."

It has now been established that intelligence is not matter, and that matter is not intelligent, by which the way has been prepared for another step in the general argument.

II. *The intelligent mind, which is not matter, is so connected with and adapted to matter, as to constitute, in conjunction with it, an intellectual machine for knowing material things.*

The material part of this machine was considered in the last Lecture. The frame work was briefly examined, and its leading parts and adaptations pointed out. As wonderful as the complex machine appeared, it would be an inert, lifeless, useless thing, without the mind that lives within it. The mind is the engineer which runs this wonderful engine. How complicated does the human organism appear, when to the wonderful body there is added a spirit-mind, which is so joined to the body as to live and act in every part of it, and yet constitute no part of it. This wonderful knowing power, the mind, which can think the universe through and around in a moment, is so confined within, and attached to the body as to have no communication with the material world without, only by using the body for such communication. The body is its instrument, by which it gains a knowledge of material things. It sees, hears, feels, tastes and smells through the organs of the body. All primitive ideas are derived through the living organs of the body, by its contacts with the material world ; and yet having obtained a few ideas through this source, it can lock itself up in abstraction, and reason upon them independently of what is going on around and outside of itself.

Here we reach a fact that places the machinery of humanity beyond the reach of any known science, and beyond the ken of the mind's own knowing power. We know the fact, but the manner of that fact is hid, and no science has yet been able to approach the union of the material with the immaterial in man, so as to explain the nature of the ties that bind them together. This is a mystery for which Atheism furnishes no solution, and which is solved only by supposing that there is a God. The way is now prepared for taking another and final step in the general argument.

III. *The Intelligent Mind must have had an Intelligent Cause.*

1. Atheism cannot account for the existence of the first intelligent minds. We may allow, that in natural generation, matter begets matter, and mind begets mind ; still it will not account for the first two minds. It has been demonstrated that there must have been a first man and a first woman, and so there must have been a first two minds, or souls, to animate the first two bodies. Whence came

these first minds? Atheism answereth not, while reason affirms that they must have had an intelligent cause, which did not exist if there be no God. Nothing short of an intelligent cause could produce intelligent minds. Allowing that matter existed, it could not have produced intelligence. Matter is not intelligent, has no intelligence in and of itself, and therefore it could not produce intelligence; and could not impart intelligence, for the simple reason that it had none to impart.

Were it allowed, for the sake of the argument, that the thirty thousand accidents necessary to the accidental production of the human body actually occurred, the mind would remain unaccounted for. Matter could not produce intelligence in any conceivable manner. One universal law governs; like produces like; every effect must have a cause, which, in nature, corresponds to itself, and no cause can produce an effect greater than itself; matter, therefore, could not have produced mind. To deny this, would break up the foundations of philosophy. Mind, therefore, cannot be accounted for, if there be no Creator. The argument might be safely left here, for no sophistry can subvert its foundation, so securely laid in universally admitted philosophy. But further investigation will more fully expose the absurdity of every attempt to account for the existence of intelligence upon the Atheistic theory.

2. It was demonstrated in the preceding Lecture that the human body must have had an intelligent

Creator. It was shown that the first human bodies could not have been eternal, could not have been produced by any law of progress in nature, and could not have been the result of accident. But we have now added to the body an intellectual machine, not matter, but spirit ; no part of it, but joined to it, dwelling in it, ruling over it, acting upon it, and causing it to act. This mind is as much superior to the body as is the engineer superior to the engine he runs and guides. It is as much superior to the body as is the power to think and know superior to the complications of a hand organ, which plays a tune by having its crank turned, which a child can do. If, then, the body gives such undeniable proof of the existence of God, as was seen in the preceding Lecture, how conclusive must the proof be, arising from the existence of the spirit-knowing-machine, which resides in the body, and controls it, and runs it as its engine ; and uses it as a whole, or in its parts, as a means of securing its ends !

If accident or chance could not produce the body, much less could it produce the mind, with the wonderful complications of its knowing, feeling and willing powers.

3. But were it possible to conceive that accident or chance gave existence to this wonderful machine, for thinking, feeling, and willing, we must add another stupendous accident. Two such accidents must have transpired near together, as it required two souls for the two bodies.

4. Yet another great accident must have occurred, which is, that these souls so happened to be, as to be suited to the two bodies which accident produced. If either had happened to have been a little different, both accidents would have happened in vain.

5. Another accident must have occurred, which is, that the two souls took up their abode in the human form, and not in the head of a donkey or a baboon. If the whole matter was not under the direction of a guiding intellect, as the Theist supposes, the two accidental souls might have found a home elsewhere. If one had found its home in the head of a donkey and the other in the head of a baboon, there would have been no human race, as it is. We are, then, forced to the conclusion that there is a God, who created both body and mind, and so admirably adapted them to each other, with all their complications, and in this conception every absurdity vanishes, and reason is disburdened, and stands relieved.

LECTURE X.

AN ARGUMENT FROM THE UNIVERSAL IDEA OF GOD.

It cannot be denied that the idea of God is universal. It developes itself among all people, in every land and age, and in every rank in society. No one will pretend to deny that the idea of the existence of God prevails in all enlightened lands. If a very ignorant and degraded people were found on some remote island of the sea, far removed from science and civilization, among whom we should fail to discover the idea of God, it would not prove that it did not exist in their minds. It might be the result of a failure so to comprehend each other's mode of communication, as to understand the contents of each other's minds. It is extremely difficult, if not impossible, on slight acquaintance, to reach the contents of dark and degraded heathen minds, of whose language we are ignorant, and who have no knowledge of our language. Yet this idea of God is so prevalent and prominent, as everywhere to reveal itself in some form.

But there is another method of reaching the universality of the idea of God. It cannot be denied that all nations have had their religion ; and the idea of God is the first and fundamental element in religion. Those who worship idols, and make their deities, and carry them about their persons as a talisman, regard them only as representations of the Invisible Power that rules the destinies of men. The idea of God may, therefore, be regarded as universal. Atheism cannot account for this universal idea of God, which must be a universal falsehood, if there be no God. They cannot deny it, it is so well known. If they were to pretend that it is not universal ;. that some persons have been found who have been destitute of it, they could then only claim a mere exception, and the rule would stand, that men, generally, have an idea of God. Whence came this universal falsehood, as it must be, if there be no God ?

It cannot be claimed that the idea is an accident, because it is general. To say that an idea so general and uniform is accidental, is to insult our common sense. Moreover, it is clear that there can be no accident in the matter. Every effect must have a cause, and every thought that men think must have a cause. The philosophy of the mind reveals the law by which thought succeeds thought, and every thought has its pre-existing cause why it occurs as it does. Why, then, does the thought occur in the human mind, that there is a God, if there be none ? There are but six conceivable ways in which the idea of God can have been produced in the human mind, every one of which, if allowed, will lead to the conclusion that there is a God.

1. It may be supposed that the idea has come down from the first man, having been communicated from man to man, from father to son, through all past generations. This is possible, but it supposes that the first man had a knowledge of God, which he transmitted, and if so, there must be a God. If the first man did not commence his existence with this knowledge, in order to a transmission of the idea of God, he must have obtained it in some one of the five remaining sources, from whence it may be derived.

2. It may have been derived from the Scriptures. But this accounts for it, only upon the assumption that the Scriptures are a revelation from God. They abound with the idea of God, but if they are not from God, the idea of God found in them is only the idea of the several writers, and how they came by the idea is left unexplained. If the Scriptures are inspired, there is a God; if they are not inspired, the writers must have got their idea of God in one of the four remaining ways.

3. The idea of God may be the result of the mind's own spontaneity. The human mind may be so constituted as to originate the idea of God, within itself, as an original conception. It is not affirmed that this is the case, but only that it is possible that it should be so. Now, if this be the origin of the idea of God, he who denies the existence of God, denies what his own internal convictions affirm, and plays false to his own nature.

4. If there be a God, it is possible that He should make a revelation of the fact of His existence in the mind of every rational being. Allowing that there is a God, who is a Spirit, He must be able to so act upon the human mind, as to produce a conviction of His existence. But this view does not help Atheism, for it assumes the existence of God, and though it is held by many Theists, it is not urged as opposed to Atheism, but only introduced as one of the conceivable methods of accounting for the universal idea of God.

5. The universal idea of the existence of God, may be a deduction of reason from the visible universe, as its premise. This is, certainly, a conceivable method of accounting for the existence of God, and whatever may be thought of it, as the probable origin of the idea, it has been held by many learned and distinguished writers. Paul, who wrote about eighteen hundred years ago, appears to have expressed this view, when he said : "The invisible things of Him, from the creation of the world, are clearly seen, being manifest by the things that are made, even His Eternal Power and Godhead."

But if this origin of the idea of God be allowed, it must be fatal to Atheism. If reason deduces the idea of the existence of God from the visible universe, it must, in some way, contain upon its face visible proofs of the Divine existence ; and as nature cannot be supposed to bear false witness, there must be a God.

6. The idea of God may be suggested to the human mind, by his own convictions of the necessity of a higher and overruling Power. It is a well known fact that the greatest minds feel unequal to the emergencies of their being. Ignorance shrouds the mind, where knowledge appears indispensable; weakness is felt where strength is required; and doubt and uncertainty hangs over the future, just where assurance and certainty are most desirable. Indeed, without a God, the great problem of human destiny is a painful uncertainty, without any possible rule by which it can be solved. Man wakes up to conscious existence, and finds himself the subject of wants, hopes and fears; often his hopes disappoint him; often his fears mock him. He asks himself, what governs human destiny? I do not govern my own destiny, for failure often attends my best efforts, and unforeseen events transpire which blast my hopes, on one hand, and mock my needless fears on the other. Is there a Higher Power, guided by intelligence, or does blind chance direct my way from life's cloudy dawn to its dark going down; and then!—what then remains, when life's dim lamp goes out in death? O, that there were a ruling Power, almighty, all-wise, just and good; how a knowledge of such a ruling Power would relieve this burdened heart of mine! I feel that it would be a blessing, if there were a God; it would relieve this feeling of orphanage, of homeless, friendless insecurity. Reason within me affirms

that a God is necessary, and does reason affirm the necessity of what is not and cannot be? Is my inmost soul false, and does nature mock herself? It must be so, if there is no God, no ruling Power; and yet it cannot be, reason will not allow that what is not and cannot be, is necessary; there is a God.

It is not affirmed that the idea of God is originated in this way, it is only given as one of the possible methods of accounting for the idea, and he who admits it to be the true method, must prove false to his own nature to deny that there is a God.

The six only conceivable methods of accounting for the universal idea of God among men, have now been examined, and every one of them, if admitted, will force us to the conclusion that there is a God. The argument, then, is conclusive. There are but two grounds upon which an argument of this kind can be successfully assailed, neither of which is available in this case.

1. If it could be shown that the argument is not comprehensive of all the conceivable ways in which the idea of God might be originated, the argument would be overthrown, but no other method can be named.

2. If it could be shown that one of these methods might be true, without implying the existence of God, the argument would fall; but this cannot be done.

It is not necessary to demonstrate which is the true method of accounting for the universal idea of

God; the force of the argument does not depend upon a knowledge of which of the six methods is the true one, but upon the fact that there is no other method; that, therefore, it is and must be one or all of the six. It may be that they are all true methods, that each, by itself, is sufficient, and would give the idea of God, provided it had not been previously given in one of the other methods. If so, the argument is sound. On the other hand, if but one of them, no matter which, is a sufficient and the true method of accounting for the idea of God, the argument is sound, since either of them, if admitted, will force us to the conclusion that there is a God. The argument, then, may be summed up thus:

1. There are but six possible ways in which we can account for the universal idea of the existence of God.

2. If the idea of God be derived in either of these six ways, then it follows that there is and must be a God.

3. Therefore, the universal idea of God, which cannot be denied when traced to its origin, furnishes absolute proof that there is a God, and Atheism is overthrown, and Theism is established.

Here we rest the argument for the existence of God, and will proceed in a few subsequent Lectures, to demonstrate His character, and bring what light we can to shine on the path of human duty.

LECTURE XI.

THE ATTRIBUTES AND CHARACTER OF GOD.

Having concluded the argument in support of the Theistic faith, and, as is believed, established the fact that there is a God, it is proper to inquire into his attributes and character.

It is not pretended that we can fully know and comprehend the attributes and character of God. That which fully knows and comprehends must be equal to, if not greater than that which is known and comprehended. One inquired, more than three thousand years ago, "Canst thou, by searching, find out God? Canst thou find out the Almighty to perfection?"

But while we may not presume to "find out God to perfection," something may be known of God, and it is our duty and privilege to know that something. It is now too late to insist that nothing can be known of God, for two very good reasons.

1. It has been demonstrated that there is a God, and hence one thing is already known of God. It is known that God is.

2. In demonstrating the existence of God, other facts and traits have been necessarily brought to light. It were not possible to demonstrate that

God is, as has been done, without demonstrating certain other facts in regard to the attributes and character of God. The proof which has established the fact that God is, has, to a limited extent, revealed to us what he is But it is necessary to make a more distinct and classified exhibit of the attributes and character of God, as they stand revealed to the human mind, in the light of nature.

The attributes of God are properly divided into two classes, which it is somewhat difficult to distinguish from each other, for want of proper terms. They may, however, be distinguished by using a little circumlocution. They are, first, such as do not, necessarily, involve moral character, or moral right and wrong; and, secondly, such as do pertain to moral character, or moral right and wrong. The first named class will be made the first subject of investigation.

I. *God is Eternal, that is, He always existed, and always will exist.*

1. It was proved in the second Lecture, that something is and must be eternal; and having since proved that there is a God, the Creator of all things, it follows that He is the Eternal One. This position is already made sure, and we have the truth that God is eternal, as a starting point, and it gives us a ground on which we can stand, and from which we can build out new arguments, relatively to other attributes and perfections of His nature.

2. Eternity, as an attribute of God, has been defined as that element of self-existence which renders the being of God, necessarily, without beginning, and without end. God is, and always was, and always will be. This attribute distinguishes God from everything else, so that there need be no confusion, and no blending of elements with the Divine, in the discussion of the subject upon which we now enter. God being eternal, nothing else is or can be eternal; this attribute is His, and His alone, and it is incommunicable. God may render other things perpetual in existence, but he can produce nothing of which it can be said it had no beginning.

3. The eternity of God having been fully settled, it is proper to remark, that this truth does not and cannot exist alone. An eternal, self-existing being must necessarily possess other attributes corresponding to this essential element of His nature, and from it we will proceed to demonstrate other attributes of the Divine nature. All that can be proved to be a necessary consequence of the eternity of His nature must now be admitted, as His eternity cannot be denied.

II. *God is Omnipotent, or All-powerful.*

1. The omnipotence of God becomes a necessary truth in the light of His eternity. He who is eternal, and consequently existed before all things, and created all that exists beside himself, is necessarily

the source of all power. There is not a power that acts, not an energy that stirs in all the universe, of which God is not the author. Now, as God has produced all the powers that fill and stir the universe, animate and inanimate, He must possess all power in himself. This power is unlimited. It will not be pretended, that in producing the universe, God has diminished his own power, that it is now less than it was before He formed the worlds, and hung them upon nothing. That power, then, which is conditioned upon nothing but itself, it being eternal, and which can produce such a universe as this without diminishing its own efficiency, must be omnipotent, or an unlimited power.

2. The works of God furnish a clear and practical illustration of His power. The worlds, and systems of worlds, which His hand has scattered through space, testify of the power of Him who hung them there, and who imparted to them their motions, and continues to roll them round.

It has been objected to this view, that as all the works of God are admitted to be finite, they cannot prove the existence of an infinite power. This may appear plausible at first view, but it is not conclusive.

(1.) It has been demonstrated that, in creating the worlds, He produced the matter of which they are composed. This must settle the question, for it must require infinite power to create from nothing, one world, or any part of a world. If it be admitted that creation, as a mere formation, is not conclusive of the existence of infinite power, still, when it is made to comprehend the production of matter where there was nothing, the argument is absolutely conclusive.

(2.) It may not require a visible display of infinite power to produce a conviction in the human mind that such a power exists. Suppose I am presented with a hundred magnets, of which I have no knowledge. By accident I discover that one of them attracts iron. The question arises in my mind, whether the power of attraction is peculiar to this one, or whether they all have the same power. This I undertake to test by experiment. I try them one by one, and find that each one, on trial, exhibits the same power. Before I have tried fifty of them I am convinced beyond a doubt that the whole hundred have the power of attracting iron. I have no more doubt of it than I should have after testing every one of them. Such is the law of the human mind. On the same principle, a view of the works of God, without reaching infinity, may convince the mind that the power that produced them is infinite. It may be in accordance with the nature of reason, to affirm, intuitively, on sight of such vast works as the universe displays, that the power that produced them is infinite.

(3.) It may, after all, be a necessary principle of philosophy, that produces a conviction in the human mind, that the visible creation, though finite, was produced and is upheld by an infinite power. All finite power exhausts itself by its own action. Every finite force is diminished just in proportion to the momentum it imparts to other bodies; yet it has been seen that nature has lost none of its energy during all of the thousands of years it has operated; from which reason may infer that the power that rolls the world round is infinite.

The argument for the omnipotence of God may be rested here, and it cannot fail to be regarded as conclusive.

III. *God is Omniscient, or All-wise.*

1. The perfect wisdom of God, like His omnipotence, becomes a necessary truth, in the light of His eternity. As God is eternal, and existed before any other being existed, all wisdom existed in Him, and must be of Him. As God is the Creator of all things, visible and invisible, He is the author of all intelligence, and has kindled every light that glows throughout the realm of space, widely dotted with thinking and knowing minds. As God is eternal, His knowledge is conditioned alone upon His own eternal knowing nature, while all other knowledge is conditioned upon Him, hence He is the source of all knowledge, and must be all-wise. As He has made everything, including all active powers, there can be no object of knowledge which he did not make, or which does not result from what He did make; there can, therefore, be no object of know-

ledge which He does not know ; and He who knows all there is to be known, must be all-wise.

2. The works of God give a practical illustration of His wisdom. When we consider what has been brought to light in preceding arguments, that the production of the first two human beings involved from twenty to thirty thousand adaptations, and then add the necessary adaptations of every separate item of creation throughout the vegetable and animal kingdoms, from the violet to the oak, and from the gnat to the elephant, and from the minow to the whale ; and then ascend to the heavens, and contemplate worlds adapted to and balanced against worlds, with all the internal adaptations of each, and reason will not and cannot conceive that the whole has been planned, arranged, comprehended, and executed by a finite intelligence. In view of the state of things described, reason affirms the existence of an all-wise mind.

IV. *God is Omnipresent, or exists everywhere.*

When it is affirmed that God exists everywhere, it is not meant that He reveals himself alike everywhere, at all times. Nor is it meant that there is not a particular place somewhere in space, which may be called the seat of His empire, and where He dwells in a sense in which He does not dwell everywhere. Yet it is affirmed that God is ubiquitous, that He is in all places at the same time. This has now become a necessary truth, in view of what has been established, and all that is required is to show that it follows as a consequence of the facts that have been demonstrated.

1. As God is eternal, He existed before all things, when nothing but himself did exist; and when nothing but God existed, there was nothing to limit or bound Him outside of himself; He was then the whole of being, and in the fullness of His own existence, He filled all in all.

2. As God created all things, He must be where all things are; as He could not create where He was not, so nothing can exist where God is not. As God is the creator of all things, the existence of everything is conditioned upon Him, and of course can exist only where He is. The conclusion is, God is everywhere, where there is anything. If, then, God pervades all worlds, and every part of all worlds, it cannot be denied that he pervades the space between them, and that surrounds them. God cannot exist in two places at the same time and not exist in and pervade all the space between them. If, then, God exists everywhere, where anything exists, and pervades and surrounds all that exists, He must be omnipresent, for beyond all that exists there is nothing to limit His presence.

3. God has been proved to be omnipotent, and from this His omnipresence becomes a necessary consequence. No being can act where he is not, and no being, less than omnipresent, can be in two places at the same time; but as God is omnipotent,

he must be capable of exerting power everywhere at the same time, and therefore He must be omnipresent, for He can exert power only where He is.

4. It has been proved that God is all-wise, and from this it follows that He must be omnipresent. Reason cannot conceive of perfect personal knowledge beyond the sphere of existence filled by the knowing subject. But it has been proved that God knows all there is to be known, and, therefore, he must exist everywhere where there is anything to be known, and must be omnipresent.

V. *God is immutable, unchangeable.*

When it is affirmed that God is immutable, the sense is not that there is no variety in His acts or works, nor yet that there is no variety in the government which He administers over intelligent beings. The particular awards of His administration may be conditioned upon the conduct of the subjects of His government, and that being various, there may be variety in His administration, and still He be unchangeable.

By the immutability of God, is meant that He is unchangeable in His nature and in the principles that govern His actions. As He acts towards one man, at any time, so will he act towards all men, at all times, in view of the same state of facts. No one can deny that the simple element of goodness or justice, would reveal a variety, when applied by an immutable mind, to different states of facts. God would have to change, to administer without variety, in view of all unlike combinations of facts. Amid all apparent variety, God remains unchanged and unchangeable.

1. The immutability of God is a necessary truth, in view of His eternity. As God is eternal, and self-existent, he can have no cause of existence, only what is in himself, and eternal, like himself, and hence there can be no cause of change in Him. If there were, or could be any cause of change in God, it must be an eternal cause, and to talk of an eternal cause of change is a solecism, an absurdity. God, then, must be unchangeable in His own eternal nature. As God is eternal, existed before all things, and created all things, there is no power or force outside of himself by which He can be affected and changed. He must, therefore, be and remain eternally unchangeable.

2. The immutability of God is illustrated by the uniformity of the operations of nature. The visible universe appears to be under uniform and unchanging laws. All the operations of nature are now carried on upon the same principle they ever have been, so far as our knowledge extends. While perpetual changes are transpiring, they appear to be effected by unchanging laws. Uniform laws appear to produce all the changes which give useful and pleasing varieties, causing nature to wear the aspect of stability. If nature only revealed as much caprice and eccentricity as man does, in his limited

circle of action, it might be inferred that God rules by a fluctuating impulse, and with an unsteady hand, but such is not the case. If earth received one kind of seed and responded by giving another; if trees produced apples one year, cherries the second, and acorns the third; if the seasons sometimes failed to find their places; if, now and then, winter took the place of summer, and summer took the place of winter; if the moon occasionally held on to its full-orbed light, for a few weeks, without waning; if the earth should occasionally change its motion, and roll the other way for a few months, causing the sun to rise in the west and go down in the east, it might leave the impression upon rational minds that God, like men, is changeable. But nature gives no such hint, but, on the contrary, she is uniform in all her operations, and works out and develops all her changes in accordance with fixed, unchanging laws, suggesting to the rational mind, that God, who formed and governs nature, is an unchangeable being, and with this accords the word by one of the Seers, "I am the Lord, I change not."

What some have called the natural attributes of God, in contradistinction from what they have called his moral attributes, have now been considered. They have been found to be five in number, and are such as constitute God what he must be, to meet the necessities of humanity, and secure the endorsement of enlightened reason. More than this, you cannot conceive God to be, in this direction. You cannot conceive another attribute of the class, the addition of which would improve his character, or make Him more efficient, or worthy of trust. On the other hand, not one of these attributes can be ignored without destroying the very idea of God, and rendering Him, if He is not annihilated, insufficient to meet the undeniable wants of humanity. Such has God been proved to be, in the light of reason, and by the force of necessary truths. It is now only necessary to remark, such also is the God of the Bible.

LECTURE XII.

THE MORAL CHARACTER OF GOD.

Having established the Theistic view of what some writers have called the Natural Attributes of God, attention must now be directed to what they have called his Moral Attributes. Moral is that of which right or wrong may be affirmed, and hence, the moral character of God is in issue in the present Lecture.

As a starting point, it is affirmed that God is a morally perfect being, just what he ought to be, and what he must be to be God, and to fill the ideal of human reason, as God. Perfection, as here employed, is comprehensive of all conceivable moral goodness, and exclusive of all moral evil. It may be affirmed, then, that God possesses the attribute of perfect moral goodness.

I. *God is Perfect in Goodness.*

This attribute is considered first, because it is generic, and comprehensive of several more specific attributes or moral qualities, which must be afterwards considered. Such will stand revealed as necessary truths, when it shall have been proved, beyond a doubt, that God is perfect in goodness. This great truth, that God is perfect in goodness, is proved by two arguments.

I. It is a necessary truth, in the light of the attributes of God, which have been already established in the preceding Lecture.

Such are his Eternity, Omnipotence, Omniscience, Omnipresence, and Immutability. Such a being must be perfect in goodness.

The argument, which is necessarily a little complicated in detail, may be stated, in substance, in few words, and in simple form, thus: God must be perfect, or imperfect, or neither; but he cannot be imperfect, and cannot be neither; and, therefore, he must be perfect.

1. God cannot be perfect and imperfect at the same time. The words, perfect and imperfect, are exclusive of each other, so that both cannot be true of the same being or thing. That which is perfect, is not imperfect, and that which is imperfect is not perfect. God is not therefore perfect and imperfect, but must be one or the other, perfect or imperfect, and cannot be both.

2. God cannot be neither perfect nor imperfect, but must be one or the other. As he is the intelligent cause of all things, the Creator of all finite, intelligent beings, who possess moral natures, and have conceptions of right and wrong, and whose conduct is right or wrong, God himself must be right or wrong, good or evil. The contrary is impossible,

unthinkable. God, then, is perfect or imperfect; he cannot be both, and cannot be neither.

3. If God is imperfect, it must be in one of two ways: either by being a compound of good and evil, or by being unmingled evil. God must be perfectly good, unmingled good, or he must be unmingled evil, or he must be a mixture of good and evil.

4. God is not exclusively evil, is not wholly malevolent. This has never been believed by any rational being, civilized or savage. There is too much goodness displayed to admit of such a belief. Much goodness is visible, is an object of knowledge, and a substance in experience on the part of all who enjoy life. All who admit that God is, and that he is the author of anything, admit that he is the author of some good, and of course he is not exclusively evil; is not wholly malevolent. That this world was created by, and is under the control of a being whose nature and disposition is unmingled malevolence, cannot be believed.

5. God cannot be a compound of good and evil, part good and part evil. This is the only point in the argument that can be contested, and here no sufficient defence can be made against it. Keeping in mind what God has already been proved to be, the argument must be conclusive.

(1.) Moral good and evil are opposed to each other, and can never combine their power to produce the same act or result, so that it shall be the result of the power of both conjointly. Good can produce nothing but good, and evil can produce nothing but evil. On this state of things let it be remarked :

(2.) An Almighty Being cannot be, in any degree, under the influence of two such conflicting forces ; the one or the other must reign exclusively and supremely, or God cannot be Almighty. Two opposing forces cannot be Omnipotent, separately considered, or as a conflicting whole.

(3.) An Infinite Being cannot consist of two such opposing elements as moral good and evil, because it would render Him less than Infinite. If God be part good and part evil, the good and the evil must both be limited and finite, and as two finites cannot constitute one Infinite, both together must be finite, and God cannot be Infinite.

6. If there be evil in the Divine nature, it must be there as an eternal, essential, and necessary element, or it must be there by God's own voluntary choice and act, neither of which can be true.

(1.) Evil cannot exist in the Divine nature as an eternal, essential, and necessary element, for the reason just assigned. It would divide the Divine nature into two opposite elements, and render God finite.

It cannot be, for the additional reason that imperfection implies ignorance, weakness, want, or deficiency. But as God is All-wise, Almighty and Infinite, He can be neither ignorant, weak, wanting or deficient ; and, therefore, God cannot be imperfect.

(2.) Evil cannot exist in the Divine nature by the voluntary choice and act of God. As evil is not an eternal, essential, and necessary element of the Divine nature, its introduction, at any time, would imply an elemental change, which is impossible, because it has been proved that God is immutable. Evil, therefore, cannot have been imbibed by God's own volition and act.

It is, then, clear that evil does not exist in the Divine nature, as an essential and necessary element, and that it does not exist by the choice and act of the Divine mind; and, therefore, it does not and cannot exist, at all, upon any possible hypothesis.

7. If it were supposable that good and evil might both exist in the Divine nature, it would still be manifest that they could not both so act as to produce practical results. It has been shown that they are opposed to each other, and cannot coalesce; that good tends only to good, and that evil tends only to evil. To this add what also has been proved, that God is Eternal, Almighty and Immutable, and it must follow that these conflicting forces cannot receive impulse or strength from any source outside of the Eternal mind itself, from which one of three things must appear certain.

(1.) The good would overcome the evil and entirely suppress it, so that good only would proceed from God; or,

(2.) The evil would overcome the good, so that evil only would proceed from God; or,

(3.) They would counteract and counterbalance each other and prevent all moral action, so that neither good or evil would proceed from God. In neither case can it be maintained that God is both good and evil.

The principle of the preceding arguments cannot be applied to man; he being finite, ignorant and weak, is liable to be affected by different and conflicting influences, and hence, he may develop goodness under this influence, and in this direction, and evil under that influence, and in that direction. With God, who is eternal, infinite and immutable, it cannot be so, for there is no cause for what He is, and what He does, outside of His own essential nature.

Here this argument reaches it close, and it may be summed up in few words. The points which have been established are as follows:

1. God must be perfect or imperfect, or neither perfect or imperfect, because He cannot be both perfect and imperfect. These points have been made certain beyond a doubt.

2. God cannot be imperfect, as He cannot be wholly evil, and cannot be a mixture of good and evil; cannot be evil, necessarily, and cannot be evil, voluntarily; and, therefore, He cannot be evil at all, in any way.

3. As God must be good, or evil, or neither, and cannot be evil, or neither, he must be good, entirely and supremely good.

II. *The Goodness of God is Proved by His Works.*

After the protracted argument, in which the supreme goodness of God has been demonstrated as a necessary truth, it cannot be necessary to make a labored effort in the present argument. It will, however, be a relief to turn the mind from its close application to metaphysical reasoning, to contemplate a visible exhibition of the goodness of God, everywhere glowing upon the face of nature.

It may be affirmed that, throughout the whole realm of nature, convenience, usefulness and beauty, were consulted by the Divine Architect. In the combination of these three elements in the visible Universe, happiness was the end aimed at, and mainly the happiness of man, the most noble creature and crowning glory of this mundane sphere. Any number of particulars might be adduced in evidence of the goodness of the Creator, but how can it be necessary, since every eye can see, and every ear can hear, and every hand can pluck, and every nerve can sense, and every heart can feel, in the midst of the universal surroundings of God-given and heaven-distilled goodness? Blind indeed must be the eyes, deaf the ears, torpid the nerves, and cold the hearts, that are not moved, and even transported, by the goodness that nature everywhere displays, and that do not, in thought, trace these flowing streams of blessings up to their great source, the Creator. Of such it may be said :

"Fools never raise their thoughts so high;
Like brutes they live, like brutes they die."

A few particulars may be properly named as specimens, which, though it appear to lessen the view by turning the mind from the comprehensive whole to a very limited part, may serve to direct the unpracticed into the right channel of thought.

1. The human body furnishes a good illustration of the benevolence of the Creator, since every part of it has its use, and promotes the usefulness of the whole, and is so contrived as to yield the greatest amount of happiness to the rational mind that dwells within. The five senses, so called, are not only exceedingly useful, but are all sources of enjoyment. If it be urged that they are also instruments of torture, the reply is sufficient.

(1.) The liability to suffering, so far as appears, could not have been prevented without rendering the system incapable of the enjoyment which is now drunk in through these senses. Who would prefer being blind, lest he should see something unsightly? Who would be deaf, lest he should hear what would grieve him? Who would be without feeling, lest he should sense pain? Who would be without taste, lest something bitter or acrid should get upon his tongue? Who would desire to have no olfactory organ, lest it should remind him of the presence of some offensive odor?

(2.) While pleasure is the natural result of the

organs above named, pain is only the result of their misapplication, perversion, distortion, or disease.

2. The human mind, no less than the body, is formed with reference to its own usefulness and happiness. Mental phenomena is divided into three general classes, as given by intelligence, sensibility and will.

(1.) The wonderful intellectual powers of man introduce him into the boundless fields of truth as his pleasure grounds.

(2.) But for man's sensibility, that is, capability of mental feeling, he would be incapable of intellectual pleasure. Now his soul vibrates with pleasure at the sight of every object, beautiful, sublime or grand; on the hearing of every euphonious sound, especially where there is melody and harmony,—and the world is full of music,—and so may every other organ of sense be made to fill the mind with pleasure. The soul may lock itself up in abstraction, and then stir itself with pleasurable emotions with its own thoughts. Memory delights the soul with pleasing recollections of all the good that has been enjoyed and is gone; hope stretches forward and gathers joys from the future, and blesses the present hour with anticipations of all the good that is to come. Thus, by means of memory and hope, the past and future are made to pour their contents of pleasure into the cup of present enjoyment.

(3.) The will is the helm of the soul, by which it directs its own powers in accordance with the dictates of its own intelligence, and by this means commands the sources of its own happiness. But for the will, the mind would have no self-control, and could not direct itself to, or hold itself to drink from the various fountains of enjoyment ; and might wander, hungry and athirst, without once blundering upon a fountain of pleasure, or crossing one oasis in its own unguided, uncontrolled, and desolate rounds of being.

If it be said that these same mental powers render us capable of misery, it is a sufficient reply to remark :

First. There could be no happiness without them.

Secondly. There need be no misery with them ; misery is not a necessary result, but comes in consequence of an abuse or perversion of these powers.

Thirdly. Those who raise the objection that these mental powers are sources of evil rather than a blessing, would not be willing to part with them in their own case, were it possible. Who would be willing to have his own intelligence extinguished, to prevent or to erase his knowledge of evil ? Who would be willing to have his sensibility removed from his soul and be rendered incapable of mental feeling, lest he should feel mental anguish ? Who would desire to have no will, to prevent his own willfulness or obstinacy of disposition ? Who would be willing to have no power to will that which is right and good, lest he should will that which is wrong or hurtful?

This argument might be enlarged to any extent, by showing that in a thousand particulars the material world is adapted to man's mental powers for the production of happiness, but the argument has been pushed far enough to answer all practical purposes, and the conclusion is, that God is perfect in goodness.

The only Objection Answered.

The only objection which ever has or ever will be urged against the entire view which has been given of the goodness of God, is founded upon the fact that evil, both physical and moral, does exist, and that good and evil mingle in human experience. Here the heathen have sometimes blundered; seeing good and evil in the world, they concluded that there was a good and evil principle in the Deity, and that the good principle produced all the good, and that the evil principle produced all the evil. This has already been proved impossible. But in further reply to the objection, let it be remarked:

1. Much of the evil complained of, undeniably results from man's own wrong actions, which are voluntary on his part, and which he might avoid, or from which he might refrain. This all men practically admit, by applauding or censuring their fellow-beings, as they judge their actions to be right or wrong. If all men would do right, do as well as

they might do, a thousand streams of evil would be dried up.

2. If all the evils which result from the wrong actions of men were removed, nothing would remain which could be proved to be inconsistent with supreme and universal goodness. In such case there would be no moral evil, no crime, and no guilt; and how much of physical evil would exist in the shape of suffering attendant on the dissolution of our physical organism in death, it may not be possible to determine; yet it cannot be denied, that if there were no violations of physical laws, physical suffering would be much less than it is, and death itself, occurring in old age, might be with such a gradual wearing out of the physical organism as to be attended by no dissolving pangs.

3. As it now is, it cannot be denied that the evils which men suffer, tend to restrain them from vice. If there were no suffering connected with this life, and especially none connected with vice, it is impossible to calculate how wicked our race would become. The fact of life's ills, and of its certain and speedy termination in death, may serve greatly to lessen our attachment to this world, and thereby restrain our evil propensities, and check our worldly ambition, which too often, as it is, has desolated whole lands, and caused nations to groan.

4. Death itself, which worldly minded men regard as the greatest of all human ills, may be, for all we do or can know from the light of nature, the

greatest good that can overtake humanity. There are pervading all minds, thoughts of a future state, and if there be a future life, death itself, with its dark and dreaded surroundings, must be the passage through which we enter upon that life ; and if it were divested of all the fears and terrors with which conscious guilt has armed the dying hour, death might not be regarded as a positive evil. But as it is, death may be a very useful admonition to the living, and a blessing to such of the dead as live in accordance with the dictates of their own intellectual and moral natures. These views are not given as Christian Theology, but only as Natural Theology, the deductions of reason from what is seen and known of God through His works, and the conclusion is, that God is good, without mixture of evil, and that what real evil there is in man's experience is the result of his own erratic course, in wandering from the way of right, and the path of duty.

Having now established the fact of the Divine goodness, a ground has been secured in which other attributes can be seen as necessary truths.

II. *God is just.*

We cannot conceive that God is otherwise than just, since it has been proved that He is perfectly good. No unjust being can be perfectly good, as goodness is comprehensive of justice, and hence, as God is perfectly good, he must be just.

1. Justice is that virtue which gives to every one

just what is due. To withhold what is due, what may be claimed as a right, would be unjust, but to bestow more than can be claimed of right, is not necessarily unjust. We see a man withhold from his fellow man what is his, and we say he is unjust; and we see another man bestow upon his less fortunate fellow man, not only what is his right, but even what he could not claim as his right, and we say he is more than just, he is generous, he is benevolent, and we approve of his conduct. We do not think of accusing him of injustice, because he bestows more than strict justice could claim. The reason is, what he gives more than justice requires, is his own, and he has a right to dispose of it in the way he does. The same is true of God's administration.

2. Justice requires such retribution for evil deeds, and such only, as is for the benefit of the whole. Reason cannot approve of purely vindictive punishment, nor can it be made to appear from what we can see and know of the Divine administration, that God ever inflicts such punishment. Justice could not allow a whole social compact to suffer damage, including the innocent, for the purpose of securing the evil doer from the painful consequences of his own wrong acts. Justice demands that the wicked suffer so much for their sins as the general good requires. It appears to be upon this principle that God has established the laws of nature, which govern both matter and mind.

It is better for the idle to suffer hunger, than that they should reap a harvest without sowing ; better for the whole.

It is better for the whole community, that the glutton, the drunkard, and the debauchee should be afflicted with disease, than that men should be able to practice these vices with impunity. The same must be true of God's punitive administration ; God's goodness and justice must unite to inflict such punishment on evil doers as the good of all demands. So much, reason affirms, and so much, justice must require, and will administer, either in this world or in the next, or in both.

III. *God is truthful.*

A statement, to be true, must be in conformity to what has been, what is, or what will be, as it may refer to the past, the present, or the future. Truthfulness may be predicated of actions as well as of words. Truth and falsehood may be acted as well as spoken.

As God has been proved to be perfect in moral goodness, He must be truthful, as not to be truthful would render Him imperfect. No argument can be necessary to establish this point. It is morally impossible that God should possess entire moral goodness and not be truthful. The truthfulness of God may be regarded in two points of light.

1. If God has made, or ever shall make a revelation to men, it must be true. The Bible professes to be

a revelation of the will of God to man, but it is not the work of Natural Theology to decide whether it does contain such a revelation or not ; it can only affirm that if it be a revelation from God, it must be true.

2. The truthfulness of God must be revealed in the complete harmony of His works, so far as we can comprehend them. There can be no contradiction between one truth and another truth, hence, what are called the laws of nature must be a perfectly harmonious code in themselves, and would so appear, if we perfectly understood them. This gives to science absolute validity. Reason never asks the question, is science true? It knows that it is true. It only asks the question, what is science? or is this science? or does science teach this or that? Men often misapprehend the laws of nature, or mistake the teachings of nature, and when they do, they falsify science, or understand as science what is not science. All real science is the voice of God speaking through His works, and must be true, for God could no more act a falsehood than he could speak one. Two things are, then, certain ; first, all science is true ; and secondly, no two sciences can contradict each other. Where reason can detect a contradiction, it knows there is falsehood ; and when the laws of nature, or two sciences appear to contradict each other, there is and must be a misapprehension of the teachings of nature. This view of the truthfulness of God is undeniable, in the light of reason,

and here we leave this attribute, without further remarks.

IV. *God is forbearing, or long-suffering.*

By this is meant, that God does not punish offenders so soon as they offend, and to the extent their offence deserves. It is not affirmed that God does not finally punish the guilty according to their demerit, but only that He forbears, at least for a time. This fact is a matter of experience, or it is deducible from what is seen and known by observation.

1. Men do wrong, and deserve punishment. This statement rests upon the universal conviction of mankind. The idea of right and wrong is a universal idea. It is not confined to Christians, or civilized communities, but is common to all classes, even the wildest of savages, and the darkest of heathen, have their ideas of right and wrong. Men differ widely as to what is right and what is wrong, but they all agree that some things are right, and that some things are wrong; that some actions of men are right, and others wrong. Some few may be found, who, to sustain a theory, will deny that men are responsible for their actions, or that they render themselves guilty and ill-deserving, by what is called wrong in human conduct; but such, if any there are, are a small fractional exception of mankind, and affirm what is so at variance with their own and everybody else's convictions, that their affirmations weigh nothing, as an argument.

Moreover, let any one trespass upon what they call their rights, and they will be as loud as any in their complaints of wrong, and will insist as strongly upon the guilt of the offender. The universal conscience of mankind declares that there is guilt and ill-desert, where there is intelligent and voluntary wrong-doing.

2. Justice does not at once overtake the wrong-doer; at least, in many cases it does not, and often it delays long, as men reckon time. In all such cases, God bears with them, or forbears to punish them, and he must be forbearing or long-suffering. So far, known facts talk, but beyond this, unaided reason sheds but little light. The doctrine of pardon is not taught in nature, and hence is unknown in Natural Theology. The fact of forbearance does not prove or ensure a pardon, because there may be a reason for delay, in the divine perfect knowledge, and reason cannot know that judgment will not be meted out in the future. If it could even be known that no punishment is awarded evil-doers in this life, it would not prove that God overlooks or pardons sin, since He may punish it in a future state, for all that reason can know, without a revelation of the mind of God on the subject.

All, then, that can be known from the state of facts before us is, that God is forbearing, and here let the subject rest; and here the argument on the subject of the moral attributes of God is closed.

LECTURE XIII.

GOD'S MORAL GOVERNMENT.

What remains to finish our Science of Natural Theology, is to point out the obligations and duties of men, as they stand revealed to the human understanding and conscience, in the light of all that has preceded.

Before attempting to exhibit specific duties, certain preliminary principles must be considered, by which a ground will be revealed, in which these duties can be seen, and their claim be more forcibly felt.

I. *God is, and can but be, a Moral Ruler.*

A moral government is a government maintained over mind, as mind, and not over matter, or over mind as matter. Physical and moral government are so distinct from each other as not to be confounded. The distinction is recognized by all rational minds. A physical government is the government of force over matter, in which the governed object has no part, no choice, no responsibility, no merit, no blame. No man ever thought a rock praiseworthy for rolling down hill, or censurable for bruising his limbs, if he stood in the way of its descent.

A moral government is a government over mind, which possesses intelligence, moral sensibility, and will, rendering the governed free in, and responsible for, his actions. Such a government is a government by motives, which act, not as gravitation in the rock, but which, while it moves the mind to act in a given way, leaves it free to act in that way or in some other direction. This fact will be more fully noticed under a subsequent division.

That God is a moral governor is a necessary truth, in the light of what He has been proved to be.

1. God is intelligent, is all-wise, and hence comprehends all causes and all effects, from beginning to end, and must know all the consequences of both virtue and vice, to individual actors, and to the whole moral system.

2. God has been proved to be perfectly good, and perfectly just. These attributes have been so clearly and irrefragably established, that nothing need be added on the subject, more than to apply the facts to the case in hand.

3. In view of the fact that God is perfect in wisdom, goodness and justice, reason cannot conceive that He is indifferent to the conduct of His rational creatures, by which their happiness and misery are affected. To suppose this, would be to attribute to God conduct which is universally condemned in mankind. Every person is held responsible to wish

well to his fellow beings, by the universal judgment of mankind, and simple indifference is regarded as a moral defect, or crime. Reason, then, cannot attribute the same state of mind to God.

The goodness of God must interest Him in the happiness of His creatures, and His justice must take cognizance of the relative actions of men, as men are just or unjust to their fellow men.

4. As God is not an indifferent spectator of the moral conduct of men, so he cannot be a passive beholder of His own moral universe, everywhere alive with activity, for weal or wo. Just what, how much, or in what manner, God should do to prevent wrong and misery, and to promote right and happiness, reason cannot determine, because it cannot know all the facts, and all the consequences, as God comprehends them ; yet this does reason affirm, that God must do all that He can do, consistently with His own perfect nature, and the greatest good of His whole moral universe. That a perfect God should do less than this, it is not possible for reason to believe.

5. No valid objection can be urged against these views, growing out of the fact that wrong and misery do exist. It cannot be proved that God could prevent the wrong and misery that exist, without preventing the right and happiness that exist. The theory now being elaborated, assumes that man is a free moral agent, which fact shall soon be proved beyond a doubt. Until the point is

reached, let it be taken for granted. None but such a moral agent can perform a morally right or wrong act, and hence, none other could be the subject of a moral government ; and such a moral agent is and can but be capable of abusing his moral freedom, and of producing sin and misery. Without freedom, by which wrong can be done, there could be no moral action, no moral virtue, no moral nature, no moral government. God stands justified in the light of reason, in creating just such a race of beings, on the following ground.

(1.) God could produce no other race of beings that could glorify Him as rational beings, be virtuous and happy, and constitute the subjects of a moral government under Him. Without the freedom and power of will which renders evil possible, there could be no moral character, and hence no display of God's moral character, in creation and government, no moral obedience, no worship, no praise, and rational happiness, based upon virtue. No obedience, no worship, and no praise is valid in the sight of God which is not free, and which is not chosen ; and the power to choose, and the act of choosing, imply the possibility of a different choice and a different course of action. The power to obey, worship, and praise God, cannot exist without the power of refusing to obey, worship and praise Him. The power to do right, in a moral sense, cannot exist without the power to do wrong. It is absolutely unthinkable. No man can think of the power to perform morally right actions without power to perform morally wrong actions. We can think of a disposition to do right without a disposition to do wrong; or we can think of a disposition to do wrong without a disposition to right; but the power to do right and to do wrong inhere together in man's moral nature.

2. God may have seen that any other race of beings, possessing the same elements of an intellectual and moral nature, would render themselves just as perverse and miserable as the human family has done. When man first sinned, God may have seen that nothing would be gained by exterminating him and creating another race, with the same mental and moral nature. This, certainly, is all possible, and no one can prove that it was not so. Allow that it was so, and the Divine mind chose between withholding His creative power, and retaining within His own eternal being, all knowledge, all moral goodness, and all rational happiness, or of diffusing them abroad through a wide-spread moral system, with the liability to, or even certain knowledge of all the evils that pervade the moral universe. So far reason safely conducts us; and upon the state of things now reached, let one remark more be made.

(3.) The all-wise mind may know that such a moral system, notwithstanding all the evils that attend it, will, ultimately, result in more good, and rational happiness to the great whole of moral being, than it will in wrong and misery. If all this is so, the great Author of the moral universe stands vindicated in the light of reason, whatever evils may be seen and felt.

The main proposition under discussion is, that God is, and can but be a moral Ruler, and that He does maintain a moral government over His intelligent creatures. The fact has been proved, and the objection founded on the existence of evil, has been thoroughly answered, and the way is prepared for another step in the main argument.

II. *Man is and can but be a Subject of God's Moral Government.*

This, of course, has been implied in demonstrating the fact that God is a moral governor, but there is a weight of direct proof which needs to be considered.

1. Man's relation to God clearly brings him within the divine jurisdiction. If man was a child of accident, an offspring of chance, the question might be raised, whether or not accident or chance must not possess the right to govern him. Even if chance produced man out of matter that previously belonged to God, a metaphysical lawyer might contend that the change was so great, and that it so affected the identity of the property as to render God's claim doubtful, if it does not vitiate it altogether. But there is no ground for any such cavil; it has been proved that God created all things, and is the

absolute proprietor of all things. God being the Author of humanity, the Creator of both body and mind, with all their powers, He has a right to govern, and the supreme jurisdiction must be His.

2. Man clearly possesses those powers which make him accountable for his conduct, and constitute him a fit subject of a moral government.

(1.) Man possesses intelligence ; he is a knowing power, and perceives, conceives, understands, judges, and reasons. Without this intelligence, man would not be accountable, and could not be governed, only as matter, or at most as a brute, by force.

(2.) Man, in the exercise of his power to know, has a knowledge of right and wrong. This knowledge is absolutely universal among men ; all men know that some things are right, and that some things are wrong. They often misjudge, and judge differently in regard to which is right and which is wrong, but all agree that some things are right, and that some things are wrong ; and all agree in some things relatively to what is right and what is wrong, and this is sufficient to render them accountable, and to bring them within the jurisdiction of a moral government.

(3.) Men have moral susceptibility, which causes them to feel a pleasing self-satisfaction, when they do what they believe to be right ; and self-dissatisfaction, or condemnation, when they do what they believe to be wrong. This element is called conscience, in common language. Some have called it a moral sense. It is better called a moral susceptibility, in this place, because it is a capability of moral feeling, and which causes the mind to feel as above stated, when its own idea of right and wrong is applied to its own actions. This is universal, for though it manifests itself much stronger in some than in others, all feel more or less of it. Sometimes the sense of guilt deepens into remorse, more terrible than bodily suffering. If this proves no more, it proves that all men think themselves accountable for their conduct, whatever their pretended creeds may be.

(4.) Men are endowed with the power of willing, or of free choice. As this is a vital truth, a brief statement of the principal proof shall be given.

First. The very common, if not the universal convictions of mankind, furnish strong proof that the will is free. We know this conviction exists in our own minds, and we see undeniable signs of its existence in others. This conviction of mankind has impressed itself upon all languages. Our plain English word, *will*, with its equivalent in all known languages, denotes a free, self-acting and self-deciding power of the mind. If it does not signify this, no definition ever has or ever can be given of it, as a simple power or activity of the human mind. It can be nothing else that is definable.

So with all its derivations, as willful, willing, and several others. Deny the self-acting power of the will, and such words have no definable sense.

The same is true of all its synonyms, such as, to determine, to resolve, to purpose. These and like words have no definable meaning, as mental acts, if the will is not a free self-acting power of the mind.

If, then, the idea of free choice has impressed itself upon all human languages, it must be a universal idea. The will is defined to be, "that faculty of the mind by which we determine either to do or to forbear an action; the faculty which is exercised in deciding among two or more objects, which we shall embrace or pursue." Deny that we have a self-determining power in the will, and this standard definition is exploded, and we shall determine, forbear, and decide nothing. If the will is not free, the power that determines is not in or of the mind; it is no faculty of the mind, as the definition affirms.

Secondly. The universal consciousness of mankind also proves the freedom of the will. Consciousness is the knowledge which the mind has of its own acts and states. When a man thinks, he knows that he thinks, when he experiences mental feeling, he knows that he feels, and when he wills he knows that he wills. No man is conscious of any restraining or controlling power by which his choice is rendered unfree. Every man, when he wills, feels and believes that he acts freely, and that he might will differently, and of this feeling and belief he is conscious.

Thirdly. Every man's conscience bears witness

within him, that he acts freely, that his will is unrestrained. Conscience has been explained. When men do what they believe to be wrong, they feel guilty, but they always discriminate between free and necessary actions, between intentional and unintentional actions. A man performs a given act in obedience to the decision of his will, and he feels guilty ; in another case, he performs the same act, securing the same result, but without the decision of his will, by accident or by some irresistible force that moves him, and he feels no guilt. Herein conscience furnishes absolute proof that the actor believes that his will is free, whatever his wordy declarations may be on the subject.

Fourthly. All men practice upon the assumption that the will is free, whatever their pretended belief is on the subject. It has been shown that all men have their ideas of right and wrong. When they see a man do what they call a wrong act, they blame him ; in which they act upon the assumption that he acted freely, and might have acted differently. Also, all men, in judging of the actions of other men, discriminate between voluntary and involuntary acts ; in which they act upon the assumption that the will is free, in what are called voluntary acts.

It has been fully proved that men are accountable for their conduct, and, of course, accountable to God. God is a moral Ruler, and man a fit subject for moral rule.

The way is now prepared for the great question, namely: What does God require of men? If this can be answered, man's duty will stand revealed. In view of all that has been proved, it will not be denied that it is God's right to command, and man's duty to obey. The will of God, in whatever way it is made known, so far as it is known, must be man's supreme law.

It is not pretended that the light of reason, in our circumstances, is sufficient to discover all that it is desirable and needful for us to know. Such an assumption would render a revelation, such as is supposed to be contained in the Scriptures, unnecessary. But while the writer entertains no doubt of the Divine origin of the Scriptures, and of their necessity, in order to sufficient religious knowledge, it is not his work in this place, to vindicate the claims of the Scriptures, on one hand, or to show the insufficiency of Natural Theology on the other. It is undeniable, from what has been proved, that some duties may be known in the light of reason, and to point out such duties is the work that remains to be done. Man being, as has been proved, a responsible moral agent, and sustaining a relation to God as his Creator, and to man as his fellow-creature, his duties must be of three classes, namely: such as regard God directly, such as regard his fellow-men, and such as regard himself. But the consideration of these duties must be reserved for another lecture.

LECTURE XIV.

THE DUTIES WE OWE TO GOD.

The duties we owe to God have been explained to be such as have primary reference to Him. These duties are now to be inquired after, as they may be apprehended by Reason.

I. *Reason affirms that it is our duty to seek all possible knowledge of God; to know God to the extent He may be known by us.*

1. The idea of God having been developed in the mind must be the most important of all subjects which come within the range of human knowledge. For any man to admit that there is a God, and then to deny that it is his bounden duty and highest interest to know what is to be known of God, is to insult his own reason.

2. The knowledge to be sought of God embraces a knowledge of His character, what He is, and what His will is concerning us.

3. This duty is discharged only when all the means of knowing God within our reach are exhausted.

(1.) The principal means must ever be mental

application to the subject ; the will should hold the intellectual powers to think, to reflect, and deeply to study the subject.

(2.) Every source of light must be investigated, and all possible knowledge drawn therefrom. The works of nature are a wide field for thought to explore.

As God is All-wise and Omnipotent, it cannot be reasonably denied that He can make in any way He pleases, through men or otherwise, a special revelation of His will concerning mankind. This must impose on the human mind the solemn duty of investigating whatever claims to be a revelation from God, so far as to reach its most enlightened and entirely honest decision concerning the validity of such claim. If reason decides against such claim, with such decision duty ends in that direction ; if reason decides in favor of such claim, its contents must be studied and followed as the rule of duty on all subjects of which it treats. All this is too reasonable to be denied. The rule, of course, demands a thorough investigation of the claims of the Christian Scriptures, by all men to whom they become known. If men cannot believe the Scriptures, after a thorough and candid investigation, they must hold themselves open to conviction, and ready to receive any revelation which God may see fit to make of His will. In view of the undeniable facts that have been developed concerning God, in preceding Lectures, for men to assume that God cannot or will not make a revelation of His will to men, and then refuse to consider the claims of everything presented as a revelation, is most unreasonable. God must be able to make a revelation of His will, and if He has not done it, He may do it. Natural Theology, then, does and must teach that it is the duty of men to seek for a knowledge of God and of His will, in the diligent use of all possible means of such knowledge.

II. *Reason affirms that it is our duty to love God.*

1. As God now stands revealed perfect in goodness, Reason affirms that He ought to be loved by all His intelligent creatures.

2. In view of the relation we sustain to God, as the workmanship of His creative skill, the subjects of His upholding and preserving care, and the recipients of His continued bounty, Reason affirms that we ought to love Him.

3. In view of the capacity and tendency of the human soul to love, by which the affections seize upon and love minor and perishable things, Reason affirms that we ought rather to love God, or to love Him with a more ardent and life-controlling love.

To deny this, would be to falsify reason.

III. *Reason affirms that it is our duty to worship God.*

1. Worship is here used in a very general sense, to comprehend honor, adoration, thanksgiving and praise. These are mental activities, and constitute

the moral elements of worship, without which all forms and attitudes of worship can have no value in the sight of God. True worship is both intellectual and emotional, and stirs the soul with a joyful feeling, in proportion to the clearness of the view obtained of the Divine character, and the intensity of the love with which the object of worship is regarded.

2. Worship will be varied in its combinations, and in its spirit and visible manifestations, according to the clearness and correctness of the views, general intelligence, and refinement of the worshipers. Christian worship, tempered as it is by the firm belief that God is reconciled in Christ, through whom Divine mercy and grace flow to every believing heart, is likely to be mild, gentle, peaceful, soothing and tranquilizing. Heathen worship, performed by rude and undisciplined minds, full of error in regard to the character of God, is likely to wear a rougher exterior, and to stir the darker passions of the soul. In Christian worship, love, gratitude and praise, are likely to predominate; in heathen worship, fear, awe, dread, admiration and wonder, are likely to be the ruling elements.

3. The worship of God stands confessed as a duty, by the almost, if not quite, universal convictions of mankind. In Christian lands there may be found one in a thousand, perhaps not more than one in ten thousand, who will deny that there is a God, and who will, consequently, deny all religion and all wor-

ship, but it is probable such falsify their own convictions. But most men will admit that they ought to worship God. Even Deists, and men who repudiate Christian worship, say they worship God in their way, that they adore Him in their hearts.

If we pass to the heathen nations, we shall find temples, and altars, and religious rites and forms of devotion, and worshipers. Their worship is rude and very unreasonable, but it furnishes no less proof of the common conviction of mankind, that God ought to be worshiped.

IV. *Reason affirms that it is our duty to make prayer to God.*

Prayer is the language of want, which is felt by all rational human beings, and which is reasonable and appropriate to be addressed to God when He stands revealed to the mind as an Infinite, Benign, and Overruling Power. Prayer is associated with worship in the practice of all religions, but it is of such vital importance, as to entitle it to be noticed as a specific duty.

2. As God is the admitted author and giver of all good things, and as we are dependent recipients of His bounty, nothing can be more reasonable than that we should, in a reverential and worshipful manner, ask Him for such things as we desire, and as we believe He is willing to give.

3. Such an association, in the mind, of asking with receiving, held there by the daily exercise of

prayer, must be promotive of devotion, gratitude and trust.

4. The fact that prayer is common to all religions, and has ever been, in all lands and ages, cannot be accounted for only by supposing that it is a dictate of reason, or that it results from the spontaneity of man's religious nature.

V. *Reason affirms that it is our duty to trust in God.*

1. In our own consciousness of ignorance and weakness it appears so natural to trust, where intelligence affirms help and safety, reason has but little to do in the premises, more than to affirm the trustworthiness of God. When other things appear equal to the intelligence, so self-distrustful is humanity, that trust in God appears like the impulse of nature, grasping for life, safety and happiness.

2. It is universal in human experience, and hence, it must be true in the philosophy of our religious nature, that men feel themselves able to trust in God, with an assurance proportioned to their own consciousness of having done the will of God.

The attention which has been devoted to the above named five specific duties, as due to God, is not to be understood as implying that there are no other duties of the same class. Some of them are generic, comprehending other specific duties unnamed, and all of them may imply other duties, so that when one is admitted, the other must be. Yet the above outline is sufficient for all practical purposes. If men will embrace these duties in the earnest sincerity of their hearts, they will not wander fatally, for want of a more exhaustive list of the duties they owe to God.

LECTURE XV.

RECIPROCAL RIGHTS AND OBLIGATIONS BETWEEN MAN AND MAN.

The subject of the present Lecture is the duties which man owes to his fellow-man. These can be revealed and comprehended, as a branch of Natural Theology, only in the light of the reciprocal rights and obligations between man and man.

Rights and obligations are always reciprocal, as seen by the eye of reason.

If one man has a right to live, all other men must be under obligation to let him live, and no other man can have a right to do what, or to withhold what will prevent his living.

If one man has a right to the possession and use of any thing, all other men must be bound to leave him in the undisturbed possession and enjoyment of the same.

If one man has a right to any enjoyment, physical or mental, all other men must be under an obligation to allow him to enjoy the same undisturbed.

No two rights and no two obligations can exist in opposition to each other; and the rights and obligations of different persons, so far as they are related to each other, never conflict, but are always correlative and reciprocal. All this is self-evident, an intuition of reason.

The natural rights of men, then, furnish a ground in which may be seen all relative duties between man and man.

I. *All men have a right to life, or a right to live.*

Life is not the gift of man, nor is it self-originated on the part of those who live. Under God it has its origin in nature, and hence, the right to live is a natural right, and belongs equally to all men.

When it is said that the right to live is a natural right, it is not meant that life cannot be forfeited. He who makes it his business to destroy life, cannot have a right to live. The interests which the murderer destroys are as great, and may be greater, than are destroyed in his own loss of life; and he being the wrong doer, it is right that he should sustain the loss, rather than the innocent. If the alternative be presented, of taking the life of a man, or of allowing him to destroy the lives of the unoffending, it must be right to take his life, and hence, it would be wrong to let him live at the sacrifice of the lives of the innocent. With this exception, all men have a right to live, and man's natural right to life is a universal idea, recognized by all men. The sufficient proof of this is found in the fact that all men consider murder a crime, and always have, in all lands and ages of the world.

It is true, some will kill their enemies, but this is done upon one or the other of two grounds. They either do what their own convictions tell them is wrong, or they act upon the assumption that the enemy they kill has forfeited his life. The test of the principle is not found in the fact that some men justify, or pretend to justify the killing of enemies, but in the fact that the universal judgment of humanity condemns the killing of friends, or even the innocent. This admitted universal right of all men to live, gives us a ground in which certain duties are revealed.

1. It is the duty of every man to allow every other man to live. It is every man's duty to refrain from all actions which will destroy or endanger the life of his fellow-being.

2. It is the duty of every man to do what he can, without too great danger to his own life, that may be necessary, to preserve the life of his fellow-being. The universal judgment of mankind would condemn him who should allow his fellow to die by fire, or water, or cold, or hunger, or a wild beast, or the hand of an enemy, or sickness, when he commanded the means of preventing it.

3. It is the duty of every man to leave his fellow-being in possession of whatever he has that is essential to his life; and to bestow upon him whatever he has, not essential to his own life, which his fellow has not and which is essential to his life. The right to life is paramount, and must not be put

on a par with any other right. A man may not elevate his right of property to a par with his fellow's right to life. It would be but little better than murder to withhold food from a man dying of hunger. It may not be said that a man, having only food enough to preserve his own life, would be under obligation to divide with his starving neighbor, because two lives would be lost instead of one; but, if he has enough to preserve both lives, he is bound to divide, even if it be at the expense of painful hunger.

4. As men may not withhold what is essential to the life of another, so men must have a right to take what is essential to life, without regard to the right of ownership vested in others, provided that they do not take what is essential to to the life of the owner. A man may take food, a horse, a boat, or whatever is essential to the preservation of his life, and the universal judgment of mankind will justify the deed.

II. *The right to Personal Liberty is recognized, by reason, as a natural and universal right.*

1. Liberty, like life, may be forfeited. When a man so abuses his liberty as to endanger the rights of others, his liberty is forfeited, and may be rightfully taken from him. But this proves nothing against the right of personal liberty as natural and universal.

2. That man's natural right to liberty is univer-

sally held is obvious, frôm the fact that he who deprives a fellow-being of his liberty, is required, by the universal sense of humanity, to render a reason for his conduct. An insufficient reason has too often satisfied; and yet, no reason ever satisfied any one which did not, in his judgment, amount to a forfeiture of the right of liberty on the part of him who is deprived of it. This proves that the right to liberty is held to be universal.

Was not liberty held to be a natural and universal right, no enquiry would be made how men have forfeited their liberty; that is, forfeited what they may never have had; but rather an explanation would be demanded, how every free man came by his liberty.

3. While some men appear to have been convinced that it was right for them to deprive certain other persons of their liberty, no man ever was or ever can be convinced that he is rightfully deprived of his liberty, unforfeited by his own crime.

The cringing slave feels not only the love, but the right of liberty within him. While his limbs are bound, his mind, his thoughts, are free; and within he reads his right to be free written in the elements of his own conscious soul.

4. Corresponding to the universal right of personal liberty, there is an obligation of duty, binding every man to allow all others to enjoy and exercise their liberty unrestrained, so long as they do not so exercise it as to encroach on the rights of others.

III. *The right to acquire, possess, and use property for one's own benefit, is recognized, by reason, as a universal right.*

1. The only limitations to man's right to acquire and use property, are two.

(1.) He may not do it by any act which is incompatible with his duties to God.

(2.) He may not do it by any act, or to any extent, which is incompatible with the equal rights of his fellow-beings.

2. The right in question, under the above named limitations, is a universal idea. It has been recognized, in some form and to some extent, among all people, in all lands, and through all ages.

3. The universality of the right of property is a necessary consequence of the right of life, which has been demonstrated. The right of life involves a right to all that is essential to the maintenance of life, which is comprehensive of food, raiment and shelter, and the means of acquiring them.

4. The right of property involves the obligation of honesty, the duty of dealing honestly. It is every man's duty to leave his fellows in possession of what is theirs, unless he obtains it with their consent, and for an equivalent. To obtain it by falsehood, deception, fraud, by theft or force, is wrong, and is so regarded by all men. The rudest hunter that ever pursued game in forest, knows within himself, just as well as the wisest philosopher, that the

game he has fairly taken is his, and that no other hunter has a right to dispossess him of the same, but with his consent, for an equivalent.

IV. *It is the right and duty of every man to acquire, maintain, and preserve a good moral character. A man's character is himself, what he is,—not what he is thought to be.*

1. The right to have a good character involves an obligation binding every man not to harm the character of his fellow-man. He violates this obligation who, by any means, make his fellow-beings worse. This may be done in various ways.

(1.) By persuading them, directly, to do evil.

(2.) By throwing temptations in their way which are likely to lead them astray.

(3.) By persuading them that right is wrong, and that wrong is right.

(4.) By corrupting their minds with error.

(5.) By exciting and provoking their evil passions and propensities.

No man can rightfully perform an act, or utter a word, by which he exerts an influence on his fellow-men, which is calculated to make them worse.

2. The obligation in question is not exclusively negative in its force. It requires right action, no less than it forbids wrong action. The common relation which all men sustain to God; and the relation which each sustains to the community of which he is a member, and the advantages which

each derives from the community, lay every man under obligation to put forth all reasonable efforts to promote the good of the community. He who injures his fellows, injures the community; and he who makes his fellows better, makes the community better. Men, then, are not only bound not to harm their fellows, but also to make all reasonable efforts to make them better. This may be done in several ways, of which the two following are principal ones:

(1.) By direct persuasive arguments to do right, to practice virtue.

(2.) By the example and influence of right actions. He who practices virtue in a community does much to improve others.

V. *All men have a right to a good reputation, so far as truth and fair dealing will give it to them. A man's reputation is what he is thought to be, not what he really is; and every man has a right to be thought to be as good as he is.*

1. A man's reputation for what honesty, integrity, knowledge and skill he has, is as much his as the farm he owns, the house he has built, the money he has in the bank, or the hat upon his head. His reputation is as much a means of obtaining the necessaries of life, and of acquiring property, as is his axe, his hoe, his plow, or his harrow.

2. A man's right to such a reputation as his real character will warrant, implies an obligation binding other men to allow him to enjoy it, uninjured

by them. Slander, falsehood, or misrepresentation, relatively to our fellow-beings, by which their reputation is injured, is a crime against them.

4. The obligation reaches still further, and binds a man to correct an evil report of his neighbor, which he knows to be false or unjust.

VI. *Another comprehensive class of duties is composed of such as depend upon the sex of our race. These duties, in their outline at least, are understood and practiced among all nations and tribes of men.*

1. Chastity is, to some extent, regarded as a virtue, and practiced in all lands and among all tribes of men. There are many and fearful exceptions, but as a whole, they are perhaps as common among civilized nations as among the wild children of nature. But the point is, that the duty is everywhere known, not that it is practiced. The duty of chastity is not only personal, but also social, rendering seduction, and all that leads to it, a crime against a fellow-being, and against the community.

2. The marriage institution, and relation of husband and wife are known to exist, to some extent, among all nations. Not, indeed, anywhere in absolute perfection and purity, but everywhere sufficiently to prove that the idea is universal; so that all corruptions may be a departure from known duty, or the result of a failure to know what might be known on the subject.

3. The relation between parents and children is recognized by all people, and the duties depending upon the relation are responded to, to some extent. The destruction of young children and the leaving of aged and infirm parents to die neglected, are exceptions, even among the darkest of heathen, while they do sometimes occur among the most enlightened people. Such violations of the law of nature are more noted because they are seen and felt to be most unnatural.

LECTURE XVI.

THE DUTIES WHICH HUMANITY OWES TO ITSELF.

I. *Self-respect is a duty which all men feel that they owe to themselves, however far they may come short of discharging it. This mental activity may show itself in bad taste, and put on the airs, and hang out the signs of pride and vanity, yet there is such a thing as just self-respect, founded upon a consciousness of self-worthiness.*

1. Men respect or disrespect others as they regard their character or conduct to be worthy or unworthy ; and they can but regard themselves by the same rule.

2. It may be affirmed that every person knows that he ought to maintain self-respect, by so conducting himself as to deserve it. All men desire the respect of others, and it is not possible that we should not feel bound to maintain that respect for ourselves which we wish to receive from others.

3. We may deceive others into a respect for us, but our respect for ourselves, whatever visible airs we may put on, must be according to what we really conceive ourselves to be. A consciousness of

self-worthiness is the basis of true self-respect. The wildest savage reproaches himself, and feels degraded, when he deceives and injures his equal, or betrays his friend ; and he knows that something better is due from him to his own being, to himself.

II. *Self-Culture is a duty which is affirmed by every man's intelligence. By culture, physical and mental improvement is meant, not moral improvement, in this place.*

1. Physical and mental culture aim at an increase of knowledge and skill. These, in some form, and to some extent, are regarded as desirable, by all men, and all feel it a duty to acquire them.

2. Knowledge and skill are essential to the maintenance of life, which is nature's own impulse.

3. Men, finding themselves possessed of powers capable of improvement, and adapted to subserve the ends of life, in proportion as they are improved, cannot be entirely ignorant of their duty to cultivate, improve and develop such powers. Reason itself must commend it.

4. It must not be expected that self-culture will be manifested to the same extent, and in the same direction and proportions by all. In proportion to the degree of ignorance and savage wildness, will culture take a physical direction, because, in such a state, more dependence is placed upon physical strength and skill, for safety, and the means of living ; but in the wildest state, knowledge is regarded

as desirable, is sought as a duty, and enjoyed as a means of happiness. To deny this would be to contradict the universal convictions of mankind. No degree of neglect in the premises can prove the absence of a knowledge of the duty, because men are known, often, to neglect what they know and confess to be their duty.

III. *The maintenance of moral rectitude is a universal duty, known and felt by all men ; not only as a duty to God and to the moral system or compact, but a duty to self, to one's own being.*

1. All men have a knowledge of right and wrong. This was sufficiently proved and illustrated in Lecture XIII., while treating of man as a subject of God's moral government. Every man has a judgment of what is right and what is wrong, in human conduct ; and every man has a conscience, which utters an approving voice within him, when he does what his judgment pronounces right ; and utters the voice of condemnation, when he does what his judgment pronounces wrong. These facts pertain no less to the unlearned, and even the savage, than to the educated and the philosopher. Every man, therefore, feels and knows, that it is his duty to refrain from what his judgment tells him is wrong, and to do what his judgment tells him is right, and thereby to keep himself innocent, free from guilt. Every man knows that when he does what his judgment tells him is wrong, and brings condemnation

to his soul, that he sins against himself, that he fails to fulfill an obligation which he owes to his own moral character, or self-worthiness.

2. No valid objection to this view is found in the admitted fact that men differ in judgment, as to what is right and what is wrong, and in the fact that one man's conscience condemns what another man's conscience approves. Here the science of Psychology comes to our aid, and explains the supposed difficulty. By this science we are taught, that as is the judgment, so is the conscience ; and that the conscience is always true to the judgment in its awards, blessing where the judgment approves, and punishing where the judgment condemns. We are also taught that the judgment may be misinformed, that all the facts may not have been brought under its notice, and that it is largely affected by education. This explains why men differ in judgment concerning what is right and wrong. The idea of right and wrong exists in all rational minds, as an intuition of reason ; but the judgment, being in error, makes a wrong application of the idea, and conscience responds to the judgment. But the crime is not in the mistaken judgment, nor in the conscience which responds to the mistaken judgment, but it is in doing what the judgment pronounces wrong, and what the conscience condemns. He who does this, sins against himself.

3. To maintain moral rectitude, in the circumstances of humanity, requires a vigorous and watch-

ful effort. This arises from two sources, namely: evil propensities within, and evil influences without. These propensities ought to be subdued, and these influences ought to be resisted, and this is known and felt by all men.

He who yields to temptation, or an evil influence, condemns himself for his own weakness; he knows he ought to resist. Also, he who is under the control of his evil propensities, feels himself degraded; he knows he ought to subdue them.

4. Moral rectitude is a state of the heart, lying back of overt actions. A man can no more approve of evil thoughts, desires and purposes, than he can of the acts which spring from them. He who indulges and cherishes them, knows that he comes short of his duty to himself, and degrades himself no less than when he commits an overt wrong act. Here we bring to view what moral rectitude demands in practice.

(1.) All impure thoughts, and thoughts of pride and vanity, should be resisted and expelled from the mind.

(2.) The spirit and temper of anger should not be indulged, but be suppressed, subdued, and rooted out of the soul.

There is a just feeling of resentment, and even indignation, which may be awakened by great wrong, but it must be kept within the mind's control. The moment that it is allowed to rise above control, and itself controls the mind, it becomes a crime, and the man is degraded in his own judgment.

(3.) The spirit and disposition of revenge should never be cherished, but resisted and subdued. There is a distinction between the noble sentiment of public justice and the low, mean, cowardly and degrading crime of private and personal revenge. This difference is recognized by all minds.

(4.) Selfishness and covetousness are known and felt by all to be degrading crimes. The crime, however, does not consist of the simple love of gain, or of possession, which may be right, but in desiring that which rightfully belongs to another. When self-love seeks, or even desires to gratify itself by invading the rights of others, it becomes a degrading crime, which universal humanity instinctively condemns.

(5.) Envy, which is a feeling of discontent, regret, or mortification, on account of the success and happiness of others, is a degrading crime, and should never be harbored in the mind of him who would maintain moral rectitude.

(6.) A fretful, peevish, complaining, murmuring disposition, in view of such ills as our foresight and skill cannot prevent, is unworthy of a noble mind, and inconsistent with the highest development of moral rectitude. Nearly allied to this are those discouraging, cowardly, desponding feelings under which too many minds quail in life's battle. Our own reason demands of us that we employ all the foresight and skill we can command, to prevent and evade evil, and then, that we bear, with a manly courage and fortitude, all the ills of our allotment. Less than this is a coming short of the duty we owe to ourselves, to our own well-being.

LECTURE XVII.

CONCLUDING REMARKS.

There is a pleasure in searching out truth, though it cost hard study; and in learning and knowing there is happiness; and yet there is satisfaction in reaching the end of labor in any given direction. This satisfaction is now to be realized in the termination of these Lectures on Natural Theology, which must here be closed by a few general remarks.

I. *The scope which has been given to the Science demands a brief notice.*

1. It has been broad enough to comprehend all the fundamental principles of Natural Theology. It is not pretended that all has been said that might be truthfully said, but more, probably, would not make the science any more certain, any more easily comprehended, nor yet any more useful. It is not practicable to push any subject to its utmost limits. It may be that all truth is so connected, that any one great truth might lead to a discovery of all truth, if our reasoning powers were clear and strong enough to trace the connection, and our intellectual grasp sufficient to seize and hold the whole. No one truth exists alone, and if our mental

vision was clear enough, it might appear that any one great truth being known to the mind, it might be traced back to another truth as its antecedent, and forward to another truth as its consequent. Then these two new truths, obtained from the one, might in like manner, the one be traced back to another antecedent, and the other forward to another consequent, and so on, *ad infinitum.* To this view add the fact that we have no rule of measurement by which we can determine any precise limits to human reason, and it will appear obvious that it is not practical to push the science of Natural Theology to an extreme and definite limit. Many other truths might, doubtless, be safely inferred from those which have been demonstrated, but enough has been done to settle the science upon a firm foundation, and it is better to leave it there than to push it out to rest upon what may be regarded as doubtful inferences.

2. While the scope which has been given to the science is sufficiently broad and comprehensive to embrace the fundamental truth on the subject, it has been kept within the range of necessary truths, or such as can be clearly and certainly inferred from them.

Nothing has been assumed, and nothing has been left to rest upon less than demonstrative argument. The whole frame-work has been wrought within the ken of reason, and can no more be doubted than can the affirmations of reason. No one principle, fundamental to the science, as it has been elaborated in these Lectures, can be named, which reason does not affirm to be a necessary truth, or a fair deduction from one.

II. *While it is maintained that all the principles which have been advanced lie within the scope of reason, it is not pretended that all men know and understand them, though it might be difficult to prove that they do not.*

1. Any want of regard for the truths that have been stated, and any visible neglect of the duties that have been named, cannot prove that they are not understood ; for the reason that men often fail to regard admitted truth, and to perform admitted duties. Men even ignore truths because they do not wish to obey them, and deny duties because they do not wish to do them.

2. If it could be proved that many are ignorant of the truths and duties which have been developed in the system, it would not prove that the system is false, that those truths and duties are not founded in nature, and capable of being known by reason. It is an undeniable fact, that men generally do not know all that they might know in their circumstances. What men are found to know on any subject, be it much or little, is no proof that they might not know more. That the heathen world, generally, might have known more of God, and of their duty, had they always made a knowledge of God and of

their duty the one great end of life, cannot be doubted. In the light of this fact, let it be remarked, that the theory of Natural Theology which has been advanced does not rest upon what men know, but upon what, in the nature of things, they might know. This view clears the theory of every objection in this direction.

III. *Should any one raise an objection to the Science, as it has been elaborated, on the ground that it is an exhibition of Christian Theology, rather than Natural Theology, a sufficient reply may be offered in few words.*

1. If the objection comes from a believer in the inspiration of the Scriptures, the objection itself is a compliment which he pays to Natural Theology. He has before him a system of religious truth and duty which he affirms is a revelation from God, and on reading Natural Theology, he confesses that, as far as it goes, it is in perfect harmony with the teachings of His inspired Book. This is just as it should be, just as it must be, to have both Revealed and Natural Religion true. The only objection that can be urged in this direction, by a believer in the Scriptures, is that the doctrines and duties of the system which has been presented, are only matters of Revelation, and have not been, and cannot be demonstrated by reason in the light of nature. But it is too late for this objection now, the thing has been done; and the Christian, while he cannot

refute the arguments by which Natural Theology has been demonstrated, is constrained to confess, that, as far as it goes, it is in harmony with the Scriptures. This is enough; it is not pretended that it teaches all that is taught in the Scriptures.

2. If the objection is urged by one who does not believe in the inspiration of the Scriptures, the objection itself is a compliment which he pays to the Scriptures. That Nature teaches all that has been embraced in the system of Natural Theology, contained in these Lectures, cannot now be denied; the arguments are finished, and reason has pronounced them sound, and to affirm that it is identical with Christianity, as far as it goes, is to admit that the Scriptures teach the truth.

IV. *Admitting the entire truth of the system, and the soundness of all the arguments by which it has been supported, it does not fill the measure of man's religious wants, and hence does not supersede the Scriptures, in which those wants are more fully met.*

1. The immortality of the human soul may be demonstrated by arguments having their foundation in nature, yet it cannot be pretended that as clear views of a future state can be derived from nature as from the Scriptures.

2. The doctrine of rewards and punishments, or of divine retribution, graduated according to the conduct of men, is a doctrine of reason; but it can-

not be denied that the Scriptures give a much clearer view of the subject than nature.

3. The existence of sin in the world, and the depraved state of human nature, cannot be hid from the eye of reason, or unknown in the experience of men ; yet the Scriptures pour a flood of light on these subjects, beyond what man, in his circumstances, would ever possess without them.

4. The doctrine of the resurrection has never been recognized as taught by nature, upon which subject the Scriptures speak directly and clearly.

5. Nature, with all her lights and tongues, is dark and silent on the great mediatorial system, which the Gospel reveals. Nature cannot teach on this subject, because her lights were all created, and her tongues all commenced their play before this system of grace was developed or needed. The science of salvation through a Mediator, having its necessity in the apostacy and corruption of humanity, which occurred after the creation, cannot be revealed in and through nature. This is revealed only in the Gospel, and here Revealed Religion triumphs over Natural Religion, without subverting it, as far as it goes. Here the end is reached, and if all that has been said shall be the means of leading one human wanderer, through the channels of truth which nature reveals, to the altar of Christianity, where the fountain of salvation is ever open, and ever flows full and free, the end will be gained, and the labor more than paid beyond computation.

www.ingramcontent.com/pod-product-compliance
Lightning Source LLC
LaVergne TN
LVHW011219110826
845150LV00006B/1479

* 9 7 8 1 4 2 5 5 1 5 9 6 6 *